YORK NC

D0531012

Paradise Lost
Books I & II

John Milton

Note by Geoff Ridden

Longman   York Press

Geoff Ridden is hereby identified as author of this work in accordance with
Section 77 of the Copyright, Designs and Patents Act 1988

YORK PRESS
322 Old Brompton Road, London SW5 9JH

PEARSON EDUCATION LIMITED
Edinburgh Gate, Harlow,
Essex CM20 2JE, United Kingdom
Associated companies, branches and representatives throughout the world

First published 2000
Third impression 2002

ISBN 0-582-42452-6

Designed by Vicki Pacey
Phototypeset by Gem Graphics, Trenance, Mawgan Porth, Cornwall
Colour reproduction and film output by Spectrum Colour
Produced by Pearson Education North Asia Limited, Hong Kong

Contents

PART ONE

INTRODUCTION

HOW TO STUDY A NARRATIVE POEM

To study any kind of literature on your own requires self-discipline and a carefully thought-out work plan in order to be effective. To study *Paradise Lost* Books I and II, you need to have the following kind of plan in mind.

- You will need to read these two Books of the poem more than once. Start by reading them quickly for pleasure, then read them slowly and thoroughly. Ensure that you include time to read the Books aloud.
- Make a list of all the words which you do not know. It is preferable for you to list these words and read on rather than to look them up immediately: try not to linger over difficult words, but to seek the overall sense and structure of the passage which you are reading.
- On second and further readings make detailed notes on the plot, characters and themes.
- Think about how these Books are narrated. From whose point of view are the events described? Does your response to the **narrator** change at all in the course of this part of the poem? Would you describe the narrator as a character? (See Critical Approaches for further discussion of these issues.)
- Assess what the main arguments are in this section of the poem. To what extent do you find Satan's arguments persuasive?
- Are words, **images** or incidents repeated so as to give these Books a patterned structure? Do such patterns help you to understand the poem's themes? Consider also the use of **alliteration**, rhythm, **simile** and **metaphor**.
- Cite exact sources for all quotations, whether from the text itself or from critical commentaries. Wherever possible, find your own examples from the poem to back up your opinions. Always express your ideas in your own words.

This Note offers an introduction to *Paradise Lost* Books I and II and cannot substitute for close reading of the text and the study of secondary sources.

Paradise Lost is one of the most ambitious works in English Literature. Its author, John Milton, attempts nothing less than an explanation of God's purpose in creating humanity, in the person of Adam and Eve, and allowing them to be tempted and to fall from grace. The **epic** poem ends with the expulsion of this pair of fallen human beings from Paradise (the Garden of Eden) into the world as we all know it – a place of pain and of death.

In its opening two Books, *Paradise Lost* introduces us not to the humans at the centre of the poem but to Satan and those fallen angels who find themselves with Satan in hell, having rebelled against God and been thrown out of heaven.

Generations of readers of the poem, especially those from the late eighteenth century onwards, have found the presentation of these fallen angels, and of Satan in particular, intriguing, fascinating, and dangerously alluring. His arguments justifying his rebellion seem at times very convincing, as do his attempts to argue that he and his fellow rebels are actually better off in hell than they were in heaven. How can a creature so evidently wicked be provided by the poet with such powerful arguments? Are we meant to admire Satan? Did Milton himself find Satan attractive? What does the portrayal of Satan contribute to our sense of how we define a **hero**? Do we find rebellion more exciting than conformity? These are the questions which readers of *Paradise Lost* find themselves asking frequently. They are subject to further discussion in Critical Approaches and in Critical History & Broader Perspectives.

Of course, these questions can be fully answered only with reference to the whole work – the more you know of the later Books of the poem, the more you will appreciate what Milton is setting up in these opening two sections. Fortunately, in the second edition of the poem, published in 1674, Milton provided his readers with a brief summary (which he called 'Argument') at the beginning of each of the twelve Books of *Paradise Lost*. These allow his readers to gain an overall sense of the total narrative in the words of the poet himself. If you intend to undertake any further reading on *Paradise Lost*, you will certainly need this sense of the poem as a whole, because, as indicated in Critical History & Broader Perspectives, very few critics will limit themselves to discussing only the opening two Books. See pp. 11–13 of this Note for a synopsis of the whole of *Paradise Lost*.

Some would claim that Milton has now become unfashionable – certainly, Milton is taught much less frequently now in comparison with, for example, Shakespeare (later parts of this Note investigate in more detail the comparison between these two giants of English Literature). Nevertheless, there are many supporters and advocates of Milton who strive to keep his work on the syllabus and alive in the minds of students. For an indication of the passion of these devotees, you need look no further than the Web site for the Milton List at www.richmond.edu/~creamer/milton. Here you will find not only queries and requests about Milton's life and works from scholars all over the world, but also discussions on how to promote Milton's poetry to a new generation of students. Further books and on-line resources are listed in Critical History & Broader Perspectives.

As an illustration of the fact that Milton's work still continues to influence contemporary popular culture, one might note the number of different works from recent years, in print and on film, which are indebted to *Paradise Lost*. These include not only such novels as William Golding's *Lord of the Flies* (1954), now a classic in its own right, but Philip Pullman's trilogy for children *His Dark Materials*, launched with the 1995 novel *Northern Lights*. This ambitious project attempts to rework *Paradise Lost* for teenagers; the first volume cites Book II on its opening page.

Perhaps more striking is the opening section of Sadie Plant's book *Zeros and Noughts: Digital Women and the New Technoculture* (1997) These pages, in a book on the digital revolution of the information age, are a reworking of a creation myth, which is considerably indebted to Milton in its insistence on the inevitability of the fall.

There are also several recent films which depend upon the idea either of a lost paradise, or of sin and retribution as expressed in Milton's epic. These include *The Truman Show* (Peter Weir, 1998); *Se7en* (David Fincher, 1995); *The Devil's Advocate* (Taylor Hackford, 1997), with Al Pacino as an American lawyer called John Milton; and *What Dreams May Come* (Vincent Ward, 1998).

There are particular reasons why Milton may suffer in comparison to Shakespeare, and some of these are outlined in Critical Approaches and Critical History & Broader Perspectives, but the study of Milton will survive, not least because of the number of enthusiasts who look for new ways of promoting this study. For example, whilst interest in Shakespeare has been helped by the **parodic**, abridged version of his plays performed by the Reduced Shakespeare Company, there is a 'Reduced Milton' of a very different order produced by the scholar John Hale. He wrote an abridged version of *Paradise Lost* for his students in New Zealand, which he called '*Paradise Lost* Post-haste. John Milton's Epic Poem in Twelve Books Distilled into Twelve Minutes for Educational Purposes'. This is his version of Books I & II, reproduced with his kind permission:

Book I

NARRATOR

 Of man's first disobedience, and the fruit
 Of that forbidden tree, whose mortal taste
 Brought death into the world, and all our woe, ...
 Sing heavenly Muse ...
 Say first what cause
 Moved our grand parents in that happy state,
 Favoured of heaven so highly, to fall off ...?
 Who first seduced them to that foul revolt?
 The infernal serpent, he it was, what time
 His pride had cast him out from heaven ...
 Him the almighty Power
 Hurled headlong flaming from the ethereal sky
 To bottomless perdition ...
 But his doom Reserved him to more wrath

SATAN

 What though the field be lost? All is not lost.
 Better to reign in hell than serve in heaven.

Book II

BEËLZEBUB

 There is a place,
 Another world, the happy seat
 Of some new race called man: perhaps we may
 Seduce the puny habitants of this new world,
 That God, their foe, abolish his own works.

SATAN

> But first whom shall we send
> In search of this new world, whom shall we find Sufficient?

NARRATOR

> This said, he sat; and expectation held
> His look suspense, awaiting who appeared
> To second or oppose or undertake
> The perilous attempt; but all sat mute ...

[lift voice, teeing up for speaker following – this applies widely to Narrator from here on]

> Until at last, Satan, unmoved, thus spake:

SATAN

> Wherefore do I assume
> These royalties, and refuse to reign,
> Refusing to accept as great a share
> Of hazard as of honour? Go therefore mighty powers,
> Terror of heaven, though fallen, intend at home
> What best may ease the present misery,
> While I abroad
> Through all the coasts of dark destruction seek
> Deliverance for us all: this enterprise
> None shall partake with me.

Professor Hale's 'Reduced Milton' is not parodic, as is the abridged version of Shakespeare. It does, however, remind us, first, that one way to get to know the poem very well is to rewrite it, and second, that Milton originally planned this epic poem as a drama, a point discussed in Critical Approaches and Critical History & Broader Perspectives.

PART TWO

SUMMARIES & COMMENTARIES

Little is known about the composition of *Paradise Lost*. We cannot even be sure whether John Milton wrote the **epic** sequentially from beginning to end, or whether he had already completed what are now the central Books before composing the description of the fallen angels in hell. One of Milton's early biographers, his nephew Edward Phillips, claims to have seen a speech by Satan (now Book IV lines 32–41) some years before the publication of *Paradise Lost*. He asserts that it was intended by Milton to comprise part of a tragic drama, and there is a manuscript extant, containing drafts for such a tragedy, which probably dates from 1640. Nevertheless, the details of the process of composition of this great poem remain a matter for speculation. This is all the more unusual, in that the greater part of the composition of *Paradise Lost* must have taken place after Milton became totally blind (see also Background on Milton's Life) and would therefore have involved his dictating passages to a number of amanuenses. However, none of these left any details as to which passages were dictated or in what order.

The principal sources for the poem can all be found in the Bible, and Milton may also have had access to the tragedy *Adamus Exul* (1601) by Hugh Grotius, whom Milton met in Paris in 1638. More intriguing is the possibility that Milton had access to the text of an Anglo-Saxon poem, now known as *Genesis B*. This poem occurs in a manuscript now in the Bodleian Library in Oxford, given in about 1651 to Franciscus Junius (1589–1677), a biblical translator and a scholar of Old English. In 1653 he published a transcript of the text in Amsterdam, and there has been speculation that Milton saw this poem: he and Junius were acquainted in the early 1640s. There are certainly similarities between the Anglo-Saxon poem and the opening two Books of *Paradise Lost*, as is confirmed in this extract from *A Milton Encyclopedia* (Associated University Press, 1978, vol. 1, p. 52):

> Like Milton's Satan, the Anglo-Saxon Satan is still defiant. He stands on his
> 'injur'd merit' and claims that his punishment is unjust. Although chained hand

and foot ... he is still 'Vaunting aloud' ... In contemplating the temptation of
Man, he is clearly motivated by ... envy, yet he takes equal pleasure in the prospect
of angering God and perverting His plans ... In such respects *Genesis B* is closer to
Paradise Lost than any other literary analogue adduced to date.

Paradise Lost was first published in 1667 as an epic in ten Books, and
shows evidence of having been carefully checked by its author, despite his
blindness. After the first three issues of this edition, some preliminary
material was added. This included a statement from the printer (Samuel
Simmons) to the reader; the Argument (Milton's prose summary of the
narrative line of the epic); and an explanation by the poet of his decision
to use **blank verse** rather than rhyme.

A second edition appeared a few months before Milton's death in
1674, and this has come to be regarded as the definitive text for modern
editions. It includes poems by Samuel Barrow (1625–82) and by Andrew
Marvell (1621–78) in praise of *Paradise Lost*, and it redistributes the epic
into twelve Books, with the Argument split into twelve sections to
precede each individual Book.

This Note is based upon the 1674 text of Books I and II as included
in *John Milton*, edited by Gordon Campbell (Everyman's Poetry, 1996).
References to other Books of *Paradise Lost* are to the version of the 1674
text in Gordon Campbell's edition of *John Milton, Complete English
Poems, Of Education, Areopagitica* (Everyman, 1990), which also includes
a detailed discussion of Milton's spelling and punctuation.

SYNOPSIS OF *PARADISE LOST*

Paradise Lost does not follow a single continuous narrative line. In the
true tradition of the **epic**, the story begins in the middle, *in medias res*.
Earlier events are presented to the reader by various means, which include
dreams, reminiscences and conversations, not all of which can be taken as
entirely reliable. For example, in Books V and VI, the angel Raphael, sent
down to Eden by God to enlighten and warn Adam, tells of the revolt of
Satan against God and how, inspired by pride, ambition and envy, Satan
seduced one tenth of the angelic host into following him. This account of
the war in heaven is in sharp contrast to the description provided by Satan

in the early Books of the poem, and the difference between these two versions is a good example of why we cannot simply accept all accounts of the past as reliable.

Milton first states his general purpose: to tell the story of the fall of mankind. However, he does not begin to relate the events leading up to this fall, and its consequences, until much later. After the initial statement of intent, Book I takes up the story of the rebel angels, newly arrived in hell, into which they have been hurled following their defeat in the war in heaven. Their situation, the individual characters of their most significant members and their occupations are described, and in Book II they meet in council to decide what is to be done. Finally, it is agreed that Satan shall fly off to the new world of man (the term 'man' is used by Milton to refer to humankind in general) to see if he can strike at God through this new creation. Satan's escape from hell, his meeting with Sin and Death, and his perilous passage to the surface of our world, are then described.

In Book III the scene switches to heaven, where God delivers a long speech on the freedom of man to choose between good and evil. At the end of this speech, which foreshadows man's freely chosen disobedience and fall, the Son offers himself as the ransom for mankind and God accepts his sacrifice. Meanwhile, Satan has landed on the rim of the universe, and, finding his way in, flies down to the sun and thence to earth. In Book IV he observes the marital happiness of Adam and Eve and is aroused to a fury of envy. One of the angels observes his behaviour and reports back to heaven, causing God to send Gabriel and an angelic patrol to Eden. Satan is thus frustrated in his first attempt to tempt Eve by means of a dream, and he is expelled from Eden.

God then sends Raphael to alert Adam to the situation and to warn him. The warning is in vain, as God had foreknown it would be, and in Book IX Milton changes his tone to one of tragedy, claiming nevertheless that his theme is more truly **heroic** than the stories of Classical and Romantic epic. Satan succeeds in his design of persuading Eve to taste the forbidden fruit, and Adam also eats, determined to share Eve's fate 'not deceived, but fondly overcome by female charm'. They become intemperate, first through lust and then through anger, blaming each other bitterly.

Book X is a tale of retribution and reconciliation. The Son descends to Eden to pronounce God's sentence of expulsion, toil and mortality, tempered by the promise of ultimate victory over evil. Adam and Eve are reconciled and accept their fate with resignation. Satan, meanwhile, has not gone unpunished. Returning to hell in triumph, he is greeted by a universal hiss instead of the expected acclamation; for all his followers have become serpents, and he himself is forthwith transformed into the greatest serpent of them all.

The two concluding Books of *Paradise Lost*, which were originally composed as a single entity, conform to another epic tradition, that of looking into the future. Just as Aeneas was permitted to foresee the Empire of Augustus (27BC–AD14) in the *Aeneid*, so Adam is shown a synopsis of Jewish history down to the redemption of mankind by Christ on the Cross. Reconciled to his fate by the promise of ultimate redemption coming after so much evil, Adam takes Eve by the hand as they pass out of Eden to face the hardships of the outside world together.

BOOK I

Book I is made up of five distinct sections:
- an introduction to the epic poem, outlining its intended purpose (lines 1–26)
- an introduction to Satan and Beëlzebub, principal among the fallen angels (lines 27–298)
- Satan's rallying of the other fallen angels (lines 299–587)
- Satan's triumphant speech (lines 588–669)
- the building of Pandemonium (lines 670–798)

LINES 1–26   Introduction to the poem

In this opening verse paragraph, John Milton establishes the style and the purpose of his epic, which he expects to be the major work of his poetic career, and also calls for divine inspiration, a way of dedicating his poem to God.

The style is established from the outset as lofty and magnificent. The opening sentence, which in many editions of the poem occupies a full sixteen lines, defines the scope of the poem as extending from the fall of man to the salvation of all mankind through Jesus Christ and also places its author alongside Moses and the greatest of Greek poets. Milton's ambition is, quite simply, to do what has never before been done with poetry: a truly breathtaking claim to make for any work of literature.

In some respects, this first sentence is misleading, because the subject matter of *Paradise Lost* is not bounded by the fall on the one hand and Christ's crucifixion on the other. The poet is about to describe a narrative which precedes the fall, and will go on to describe the war in heaven, an even earlier episode. His poem will end not with the anticipation of the life, ministry and death of Christ, but includes a description, through the voice of Michael, of the state of the Church in Milton's own time.

The opening line of this epic poem is, in itself, a striking instance of poetic ambiguity. Milton tempts the reader into believing that the break at the end of the line – the completion of the ten syllables characteristic of **blank verse** – is also a break in meaning; in other words, that the first line represents a complete sentence: 'Of man's first disobedience, and the fruit.' In that interpretation, we might expect that *Paradise Lost* is to be concerned with the first disobedience of mankind and the fruit of that disobedience. Milton, however, runs the line on so that the fruit is not the consequence of the disobedience, but the fruit of the forbidden tree. Of course, the 'fruit' is, in fact, both the outcome of the sin of disobedience and the literal fruit on the tree. Milton specifically refers to an apple only once in *Paradise Lost,* when Satan, returning to hell after corrupting Eve and Adam describes what he has done in these terms (Book X lines 485–7):

> Him by fraud I have seduced
> From his creator, and the more to increase
> Your wonder, with an apple

1 **first** this word is repeated throughout the early section of this Book (e.g. lines 19, 27, 28 and 33), emphasising that this is the beginning of Milton's epic

2 **mortal taste** deadly taste, but also tasting by a human being

6 **heavenly Muse** divine inspiration, the Word (in the gospel of John)

6–7 **secret top / Of Oreb, or of Sinai** the holy mountains referred to in the Old Testament book of Exodus, frequently referred to in this opening Book of *Paradise Lost*

10 **Zion** a hill in Jerusalem

11 **Siloa's brook** a pool in Jerusalem

15 **Aonian** the mountain believed to be the home of the Greek poetic muses

17–18 **that dost prefer / Before all temples** a reference to Christ's condemnation of the misuse of the temple, but also an indication of Milton's Puritan nonconformism (see Background)

19 **Instruct me** Milton is seeking inspiration from the Holy Spirit, which was present at creation (lines 19–20), in his attempt to write his own narrative of the creation, following the biblical accounts in Genesis and John. In one sense this search for inspiration makes Milton not responsible for his epic: he is simply the mouthpiece for God, rather as the American novelist Harriet Beecher Stowe (1811–96) could claim that she did not write *Uncle Tom's Cabin*, but merely took God's dictation. Milton is claiming his own private divine inspiration. However, there is no doubt that Milton was very aware of his place as author of this epic, even if, as recent critics have noted (see Critical History & Broader Perspectives), *Paradise Lost*, like *Uncle Tom's Cabin*, is also the product of a specific historical moment

LINES 27–298   Introduction to Satan and Beëlzebub

Milton introduces the principals among the fallen angels: Satan, and his close ally Beëlzebub. He also begins the process of describing hell, a complex location (see Critical Approaches) in which the fallen angels strive to find some stability.

Milton includes a summary of the central action of the poem (lines 34–49) which traces the career of Satan back from the deception of Eve, which will be described at the end of the poem, to the revolt in heaven, which has taken place just before the epic begins.

He describes the fall of the angels who rebelled with Satan (lines 50–83) and then concentrates on the first speeches of Satan (lines 84–124) and of Beëlzebub (lines 128–55). In Satan's opening speech, his account of the war in heaven is crucially biased: we could easily believe from his words that all the angels had rebelled. Beëlzebub is allowed only a much shorter speech, which illustrates his uncertainty. He is unsure whether angels can in fact perish, and this leads him to the dreadful possibility that the fallen angels, now recovering their strength, may be condemned to everlasting servitude.

Satan's reply (lines 156–91) reveals Satan's true motive, which is always to do what is evil. He seems almost to acknowledge the infinite goodness of God in this speech, by recognising the possibility that God might seek to bring forth goodness even from the evil of the fallen angels. This idea that a fall may be fortunate becomes more significant in relation to the fall of mankind, especially in the final Books of *Paradise Lost* (see also Critical History & Broader Perspectives).

The plight of Satan is described, and his intention to make himself ruler of hell. After a brief response from Beëlzebub, which completes their initial debate, Satan and Beëlzebub make their first moves in surveying hell (lines 192–298).

28 **what cause** Milton is constantly looking for causes and logical explanations throughout his epic

30 **Favoured of** this is ambiguous: 'favoured of' means both 'honoured by' and 'resembling'

fall the opening two Books include many references to falling and to rising (see, for example, Book I lines 330–4)

34 **infernal serpent** Satan

40 **equalled the most high** this is, effectively, a **paradox**, since it is in this sense impossible to equal the highest

44 **vain attempt** this means both 'attempt which was in vain' and 'attempt prompted by vanity'

64 **discover** make visible

70–1 **Such place … rebellious** these lines raise fundamental issues about knowledge and creation – it appears that hell was always there, waiting for occupants, but the angels did not know of it

74 **from the centre ... to the utmost pole** from the equator to the pole

93–4 **till then ... arms?** Satan argues here that the knowledge of the angels was limited: they had no idea of the extent of God's power. Satan uses this limitation as an excuse for rebellion, arguing that the actions of the fallen angels were born of a desire to discover how powerful God was. This prefigures the fall of mankind, which results from a desire to discover forbidden knowledge

104 **dubious battle** a battle in which the likely outcome is unclear; in fact, there could never be any doubt about the result of this battle

105 **field** battle

111 **bow and sue for grace** these are cornerstones of Christian religious practice

126 **Vaunting aloud, but racked with deep despair** this line encapsulates the paradox of Satan's situation: outwardly he boasts confidently, but inwardly he is in turmoil

133 **Whether upheld by strength, or chance, or fate** Beëlzebub cannot concede that the power of God might be God's by right – in his view it must be a matter of chance

169–71 **But see ... heaven** this is, arguably, the first event in the poem, as Satan witnesses the end of the attack from heaven. He attributes this either to God's scorn, or to the end of God's appetite for war

178 **occasion** opportunity

184 **the tossing of these fiery waves** we are reminded that hell is an unstable place (see Themes on Uncertainty & Instability and Textual Analysis, Text 1)

196 **rood** a unit of area, usually a quarter of an acre

196–208 **in bulk as huge ... morn delays** this is the first instance in *Paradise Lost* of one of the most famous features of the poem: the **epic simile**. This extended comparison, more than a dozen lines in length, allows Milton to place his poem in the ranks of the great epics of the past as he compares the size of Satan with monsters from classical tradition. A second epic simile is to be found at lines 230–8

199 **Briareos or Typhon** giants of classical legend

201 **Leviathan** a particularly appropriate point of comparison, because Leviathan is a sea creature, and hell has been described thus far as a watery region. Moreover, he provides an illusion of stability, such that some fishermen mistake him for a rock and try to anchor on his back, believing themselves to be in a place of safety. Likewise, Satan seems to offer security to those who trust in him, a security which is equally illusory

210–20 **nor ever thence ... poured** Milton makes it clear that any action which Satan takes can be taken only with God's permission, and that whatever evil Satan may commit will bring only infinite goodness, grace and mercy from God. The concepts of goodness, grace and mercy are more fully developed and defined in Book III

232–3 **Pelorus** and **Etna** a promontory (modern-day Cape Faro) and a volcano in Sicily

239 **Stygian** dark; the adjective derives from Styx, the river of the underworld in Greek mythology

240–1 **by their ... power** compare with lines 210–20

246 **now is sovereign** Satan cannot see that God's sovereignty is not a temporary state – God is always sovereign, not just 'now'

248 **force hath made supreme** here Satan seems to believe, as Beëlzebub suggested earlier (line 133), that God has achieved victory simply through superior strength

252 **new possessor** Satan argues that, because he occupies hell, he therefore possesses it. This is a fallacious argument, but a popular view, which has been deployed by colonising powers throughout human history

254 **The mind is its own place** Satan believes that he himself can effect a kind of creation: not the creation of worlds or beings which God can bring about, but the use of his mind to render his physical state either better or worse. Gordon Campbell suggests that this is a heretical view (*John Milton, Complete English Poems, Of Education, Areopagitica*, 1990, p. 156) based on the opinions of Amalric, a twelfth-century French philosopher who argued that heaven and hell were states determined simply through one's conscience. However, a comparable sentiment is expressed by Milton's near contemporary, John Donne, in his love poem 'The Good Morrow' (1633): 'For love, all love of other sights controls, / And makes one little room, an everywhere.' The idea that hell is a state of mind rather than a physical location is also expressed by the character Mephistopheles in Christopher Marlowe's play *Doctor Faustus* (1604), for example: 'Why, this is hell, nor am I out of it' (Act I Scene 3); and 'Hell hath no limits nor is circumscribed / In one self place, where we are is hell' (Act II Scene 1)

258–9 **Here at least / We shall be free** Satan appears to believe that distance from God will bring freedom to the fallen angels. This is a belief which was paralleled in the thinking of many of those Protestants who fled Europe for the New World in Milton's time (see also Background): they expected to find freedom from religious oppression. Milton fashions, through Satan, an inversion of his own sympathetic view of these exiles, as expressed in this sentence from his first prose pamphlet: 'what numbers of faithful and freeborn Englishmen, and good Christians, have been constrained to forsake their dearest home ... whom nothing but the wide ocean, and savage deserts of America, could hide and shelter from the fury of the bishops?' (*Of Reformation*, 1641, in *Milton's Prose Writings*, ed. K.M. Burton, Everyman, 1958, p. 34). For a fictional account of Milton's views on America see Peter Ackroyd's novel *Milton in America* (Sinclair-Stevenson, 1996)

263 **Better to reign in hell than serve in heaven** in this single **epigrammatic** line, Satan summarises his entire ambition

266 **astonished** stunned

oblivious pool a pool which has the property of making all who drink its waters forget their past. Milton returns to this idea in Book I line 301, where the fallen angels 'lay entranced', and, more specifically, in Book II line 563, where he describes the Greek myth of the River Lethe, from which he derives the notion of waters of forgetfulness

268 **unhappy mansion** possibly 'unhappy state of being' rather than 'mansion' in its current sense of 'magnificent building'. Since nothing has yet been built in hell, Milton would be unlikely to use the latter meaning

274 **If once they hear that voice** Beëlzebub shrewdly draws attention to the heart of Satan's power: his voice. Satan is a master of **rhetoric**

282 **pernicious height** either a height which could have been fatal, or a height which was wicked. Beëlzebub could perhaps be suggesting that heaven was itself wicked

285 **Ethereal temper** tempered (i.e. created) in heaven

287–91 **like the moon ... globe** a further **epic simile** based upon the 'Tuscan artist', the astronomer Galileo, whom Milton met on his European tour (see Background)

290 **descry** discover

291 **spotty** spotted: the surface of the moon would appear to be spotted when seen through a telescope

294 **ammiral** a variant of 'admiral', **synecdoche** for the ship carrying an admiral
wand the most slender of sticks

296 **marl** clay, soil, earth

297 **azure** usually referring to the colour blue, but having extended its meaning to the blue of an unclouded sky. Milton is, here, the first writer to use the term to refer to unclouded vaults of heaven

LINES 299–587   Satan's rallying of the other fallen angels

This section begins with a description of the fallen angels (lines 299–315), whom Satan begins to rouse (lines 315–30). Milton then describes, at length, the reaction of the fallen angels as they respond to Satan's call (lines 331–587).

Satan begins the process of rallying the fallen angels by using flattery (as he did in his initial address to Beëlzebub), addressing them with titles of rank. He suggests two very different reasons why they might be lying here: the worthy reason of resting after battle, or the very unworthy reason of having admitted defeat.

The fallen angels rouse themselves as a result of fear, and their leaders are named and described. Milton makes extensive use of his knowledge of the Old Testament in this section, giving names to the principals among the fallen angels which are derived from those fallen gods who tried to seduce the chosen people from the true God. Towards the end of this catalogue (lines 506–21), Milton adds a secondary list of false gods, derived from Greek mythology and therefore, as far as Milton is concerned, inferior to the false gods of the Bible.

299 **Nathless** nevertheless

303 **Vallombrosa** a valley in Etruria (a region corresponding roughly to modern-day Tuscany)

305 **Orion** in Greek mythology, a hunter and giant who was turned into a constellation when he died

307 **Busiris** an Egyptian pharaoh
   Memphian from the Egyptian city of Memphis

309 **sojourners of Goshen** the Israelites

319 **repose** restore, regain

322 **abject posture** posture of surrender

324 **Cherub and seraph** the first two of the nine theological orders of angels. The standard hierarchical ordering of the ranks placed them into three degrees, or 'choirs', each consisting of three ranks: Seraphim, Cherubim, Thrones; Dominions, Virtues, Powers; Principalities, Archangels, Angels. Satan uses some of these titles at the beginning of the debate in Book II

325 **ensigns** the flags hoisted in battle

till anon until eventually

329 **Transfix** fasten

332 **wont** accustomed

335 **Nor did they not perceive the evil plight** the double negative might lead to the sense being lost here. Milton is saying that the fallen angels were very aware of their situation and their pain, but their fear of Satan made them obey

345 **cope** cloak (specifically, the cloak of a priest) or canopy. The phrase 'under the cope of heaven', meaning 'in all the world', was quite common from the fourteenth century to the eighteenth century – here, Milton makes a startling departure from that common phrase

348 **sultan** leader; in Milton's time the word would also have carried the negative connotations of an Eastern, unchristian tyrant

349 **light** alight, land

350 **brimstone** sulphur, a fiery element (see line 69)

351 **populous North** in ancient times, the threat to Roman civilisation came from the peoples of northern Europe

352 **frozen loins** a metaphor for the cold lands of the north

353 **Rhene** Rhine

Danaw Danube

360 **erst** formerly

362 **razed** erased, removed

363 **Books of Life** the books referred to in Revelation 3:5 and 21:27, which are God's records of those who will escape damnation

364 **sons of Eve** humanity

366 **high sufferance** divine permission

372 **gay religions full of pomp and gold** Milton, like all Puritans (see Background), despised religious practices which involved lavish ceremony and decorated churches

373 **devils to adore for deities** to adore devils instead of gods

380 **promiscuous crowd** a crowd unworthy to be named individually

383 **next** next to

386 **Jehovah** the name used for God in the Old Testament

391 **affront** confront

392– **Moloch ... Belial** the classical **epics** (see Literary Background) included this
505 kind of lengthy catalogue of names. The list here comprises twelve false
gods: Moloch (lines 392–405); Chemos (lines 406–18); Baälim and
Ashtaroth (lines 419–37); Ashtoreth (lines 437–46); Thammuz (lines
446–57); Dagon (lines 457–66); Rimmon (lines 467–76); Osiris, Isis and
Orus (lines 476–89); and, finally, Belial (lines 490–505). The number
twelve is the number of the disciples of Christ. Most of the names are
drawn from the Old Testament, although Milton also weaves in elements
from classical mythology (for example, in combining Thammuz and Adonis).
A similar catalogue of false gods occurs towards the end of Milton's early
poem 'On the Morning of Christ's Nativity'

396 **the Ammonite** the tribe of the Ammonites

403 **opprobrious** corrupted

   grove shady wood

405 **type of hell** image or model of hell

413 **Israel** the tribes of the Israelites

423–31 **For spirits ... fulfil** the gender of angels and spirits was a matter to which
Milton devoted some attention: he returns to it in a discussion between
Adam and the angel Raphael at the end of Book VIII

429 **Dilated** expanded

433 **Their living strength** the true God which sustained their lives

   unfrequented abandoned

441 **Sidonian virgins** virgins from the Phoenician city of Sidon (in modern-day
Lebanon)

444 **uxorious** excessively devoted to his wife

447 **annual wound** the death of Thammuz (Adonis) was mourned in Phoenicia
every spring when the river carried red mud, which the people believed to
be his blood

457 **alienated** exiled (also, having turned away from God)

458 **captive ark** the ark of the covenant captured by the Philistines

460 **groundsel** threshold

469 **lucid** clear and bright

472 **sottish** foolish

477 **crew** rabble

481 **disguised in brutish forms** Milton believes the false gods of the Egyptians to have the form of animals, rather than having the human shape of the true God

490 **Belial** Belial is generally used in the Old Testament to refer to a state of sinfulness. This is why he has no temple (line 492)

497 **In courts and palaces he also reigns** the sense of Belial as representing corruption in general allows Milton to attack courts and the aristocracy

502 **flown** swollen

506–21 **These ... isles** Milton is dismissive of these Greek gods, refusing to name them in full detail because their list is so 'long to tell', and because they inhabit several places ('in Crete ... or on the Delphian cliff ... Or in Dodona')

523 **damp** depressed

524 **Obscure** hidden

527 **he** Satan

wonted usual, accustomed

528 **recollecting** recovering

529 **Semblance of worth, not substance** the distinction here between 'Semblance' (appearance) and 'substance' (reality) is crucial. Satan's speeches to the fallen angels do not reveal the uncertainty he really feels, nor does his flattery of them reveal the true extent of their misery

533 **standard** military flag

536 **advanced** raised up

537 **meteor** comet

539 **Seraphic** belonging to the seraphs (see line 324)

540 **metal** trumpets

546 **orient colours** the bright colours of the east (as at sunrise)

547 **helms** helmets

548 **serried** tightly packed

549 **anon** immediately

550 **phalanx** a military formation

Dorian mood a simple, solemn style of music

551 **soft recorders** wind instruments with a mellow sound

556 **swage** assuage

557 **touches** notes of music

561 **charmed** possibly not a positive term here, with its connotations of enchantment and magic

563 **horrid** bristling with spears

564 **guise** disguise

567 **files** military divisions

568 **traverse** across

570 **visages** faces

571 **sums** calculates

575–6 **that small infantry / Warred on by cranes** the small infantry attacked by cranes is an incident in the classical **epic** the *Iliad*

578 **Thebes and Ilium** the central locations of the Greek epics. Ilium is another name for Troy

580 **Uther's son** King Arthur, legendary king of the Britons

583–7 **Aspramont ... Fontarabbia** the places named here are all to be found in legends and romances

LINES 588–669   Satan's triumphant speech

There is a brief introduction to Satan's speech by the **narrator** (lines 590–621), followed by the speech itself.

> Satan refuses to acknowledge God's divine superiority, describing God as ruling merely through ancient custom (lines 639–40). He goes on to accuse God of being responsible for the fall of the angels: his logic is that God concealed his own power, and therefore tempted the angels to test his might (see lines 641–2).

> The climax of the speech (lines 646–7) is in itself a neat summary of how Satan operates: he has failed to rebel against God through force, and now turns to the disreputable practices of fraud and guile.

588 **observed** gave honour to

590 **eminent** tall

593 **archangel** principal among the ranks of the angels (see note to Book I line 324)

594–9 **as when the sun ... Darkened so** an **epic simile** comparing Satan's appearance in his fallen state to that of the sun when obscured by cloud or in eclipse (see also Language & Style on Images of the Sun)

596 **Shorn** deprived

599 **Perplexes monarchs** the sun was the traditional symbol of royalty; the **simile** thus allows Milton to include a reference to monarchy which associates it with Satan and with superstition

603 **considerate** deliberate

606 **The fellows of his crime, the followers rather** the fallen angels are not equally to blame: they followed Satan

608 **lot** share

609 **amerced** deprived

613 **scathed** scorched

619 **assayed** attempted

624 **event** outcome

632 **puissant** powerful

632–3 **whose exile / Hath emptied heaven** Satan's account of the war again exaggerates the number of angels who followed him (see lines 100–5)

634 **Self-raised** raised by their own power. It is a favourite ploy of Satan in *Paradise Lost* to claim that he and his followers are capable of action independent of God

637 **he** God

650 **rife** widespread, common

651 **fame** rumour

655 **pry** like 'fraud' and 'guile' (line 646), 'pry' is a loaded term which suggests deviousness – it is hardly the behaviour we expect of an angel

656 **eruption** breaking forth from constraint

660 **despaired** no longer to be hoped for

666 **illumined** gave light to

LINES 670–798   The building of Pandemonium

This final section of Book I describes the construction by the fallen angels of Pandemonium, which will be their palace in hell.

'Pandemonium', a word now used in the general sense of a noisy, chaotic place, means 'the place of all demons', and is a word of Milton's own invention. This construction, the first of all buildings, and the first of all objects not created directly by God, is a product of hell: Milton no doubt wanted his readers to contrast this artificial construction in all its ugliness with the natural beauties of Eden and heaven.

670 **grisly** horrible

671 **Belched** Milton portrays the site of Pandemonium as if it were a disgusting human body

672 **scurf** thin turf, having the appearance of poor skin

678 **Mammon** a name used in the Bible, and later in popular tradition, to personify the love of wealth

683 **aught** anything

684 **vision beatific** the sight of God

690 **ribs of gold** Eve is formed from one of Adam's ribs

690–2 **Let none ... bane** Milton, in typical Puritan fashion (see Historical Background), despises wealth and splendour: he therefore locates the source of such display in hell

692 **the precious bane** the curse of gold: this is an **oxymoron**

694 **Babel** the tower of Babel

the works of Memphian kings the Egyptian pyramids

697 **reprobate** evil

700 **Nigh** nearby

703 **founded** melted (as in 'foundry'), but possibly also with the sense here of 'originated'

704 **Severing** separating

scummed skimmed, removed the scum

dross the waste material produced when smelting metal

711 **exhalation** breath or vapour

712 **dulcet** sweet-sounding

713 **temple** a place of worship which Milton would have disapproved of (see lines 17–18)

pilasters rectangular columns

714 **Doric** the oldest and simplest of the ancient Greek orders of architecture

715 **architrave** top beam

716 **Cornice** ornamental moulding

frieze a decoration between the architrave and the cornice

bossy rounded

723 **straight** immediately

724 **brazen** made of brass

discover reveal

727 **Pendent** hanging

728 **cressets** vessels holding fire for light

729 **naphtha** an inflammable liquid

asphaltus black resin

732 **his hand** Mulciber's handiwork (he is finally identified in line 740)

739 **Ausonian land** the Greek name for Italy

741 **Jove** the Roman name for Zeus, the Greek god who cast Mulciber (or Vulcan) from heaven. Milton whets our appetite for this story from the *Iliad*, only to declare that it is a lie ('thus they relate, / Erring', lines 746–7)

745 **zenith** the highest point of heaven

750 **engines** skills, wiles

    sent thrown

751 **industrious** ingenious

753 **awful** inspiring awe or reverence

758 **squarèd regiment** troop drawn up in squares

761 **Attended** accompanied by attendants

764 **soldan's** sultan's (see also note to line 348)

765 **paynim** pagan (and therefore, like 'the soldan', not to be admired)

766 **career** charge

774 **expatiate** walk about freely

776 **straitened** confined

787 **jocund** happy

789 **incorporeal** having no bodily form

795 **close recess** secret meeting

    conclave also meaning a 'secret meeting', the term usually refers to the assembly which elects a Pope (thus Milton makes Catholicism a product of hell)

BOOK II

Book II is made up of three distinct sections:

- the great debate itself, which comprises a number of separate speeches (lines 1–520)
- the description of the fallen angels after Satan's departure (lines 521–628)
- Satan's voyage and his encounters, especially with Sin and Death (lines 629–1055)

LINES 1–520   The great debate

After a brief introduction by Satan (lines 1–42), this section consists of speeches by four of the fallen angels, Moloch (lines 43–105), Belial (lines 106–225), Mammon (lines 226–83) and Beëlzebub (lines 298–378) as the fallen angels, having been cast into the unknown territory of hell, try to decide what to do next. It is clear that Beëlzebub offers a point of view already discussed with Satan. There is then a vote (lines 378–89), following which Beëlzebub congratulates the assembly on their decision to seek the ruin of Eden and poses the question of who will put the plan into action (lines 390–429). Satan then volunteers, and has his first substantial speech in this Book (lines 430–66), after more than four hundred lines of debate.

> Satan's introduction to the debate characterises God as 'the thunderer' (line 28). This is one example of a range of negative terms used by the fallen angels to describe God throughout their discussion. The same practice is also adopted by Eve later in *Paradise Lost*, immediately after her fall (Book IX line 815).
>
> The principal speeches in the debate are characterised by their expression of uncertainty. The fallen angels do not know what they are capable of, nor what God is capable of. They are also uncertain in the sense that three of the four proposers (Moloch, Belial and Mammon) are not taking part in a real debate: Satan and Beëlzebub have already determined what will happen, even before the first words are uttered.
>
> Moloch expresses uncertainty about what the future might hold, wondering whether the fallen angels can be destroyed, and whether anything can be imagined which is worse than hell. Belial seizes upon Moloch's uncertainty over what God might do next, and comes to a different conclusion. Belial's eloquence equips him to paint a vivid portrait of how awful the future could be.
>
> Mammon considers the possibility of God pardoning the fallen angels, and describes this in negative terms of 'Forced halleluiahs' (line 243) and 'servile offerings' (line 246) given to an 'envied sovereign' (line 244). At no point does he, or any of the other fallen angels, consider that they may freely repent, accept God's superiority and worship God freely.
>
> Beëlzebub, seeing that the fallen angels are persuaded by Mammon and are likely to opt for peace, intervenes to suggest the strategy of

corrupting humanity in Eden. He again uses negative terms to describe God, such as 'the conqueror' (line 338).

Milton provides introductory descriptions of each of the speakers, which precede their contributions. These serve to affect our expectations about each speaker's position in the debate. The introduction to Moloch, 'the strongest and the fiercest' (line 44), leads us to expect that he will argue for war. Belial's introduction, which emphasises his skilful tongue, suggests that he will be more subtle in his argument. Mammon (whom, like Beëlzebub, we have met before) is given no introduction, because he needs none: since he represents the love of riches, it is inevitable that he will argue that the fallen angels should seek to discover all the riches and resources of hell.

In accepting the task, Satan begins by emphasising how difficult this expedition will be – so difficult, that it is not surprising that there have been no volunteers. The reader needs to bear in mind that Satan's description of what lies outside hell is based purely on conjecture: nothing prepares him, or the reader, for what is to be encountered in the later parts of Book II.

In Milton's time political debates had been held in Parliament before the Civil War, among the army during the war and in Parliament again during the rule of Cromwell (see Historical Background). Milton and his readers would, therefore, have had ample experience of the ways in which arguments and proposals were made. As the debate comes to an end (lines 496–505), Milton, in the voice of the **narrator**, laments that even devils keep agreement ('concord') with one another: only the human race shows disagreement, and hypocrisy. This seems to be a comment on the disputes, both military and spiritual, of Milton's own day.

2 **Ormus** a trading city, famous for its jewels
Ind India
3 **gorgeous** showy
4 **barbaric pearl and gold** pearl and gold fashioned in an uncivilised manner
6 **bad eminence** supremacy in evil

8 **insatiate** with an appetite not to be appeased

9 **success** the outcome of his previous experience

11 **Powers and dominions** these, like 'virtues' in line 15, are ranks of angels (see note to Book I line 324)

16 **More glorious and more dread than from no fall** Satan argues that the fall will prove beneficial, in that the fallen angels will be more glorious than they were before. This is a version of the 'fortunate fall', an idea which is introduced later in the poem in relation to the fall of mankind (see also further discussion in Critical History & Broader Perspectives)

18 **just right, and the fixed laws** Satan argues that his leadership is somehow legitimate. He has argued in Book I lines 639–40 that God's leadership is merely a matter of custom

23 **a safe unenvied throne** in a brilliant piece of **rhetoric**, Satan attempts to suggest that his rule in hell is superior to that of God in heaven: because hell is so terrible, he argues, nobody will harbour the ambition of trying to remove Satan from his throne. Satan's eminence, he suggests, serves merely to make him the first target of God's wrath

29 **bulwark** defence

39 **prosperity** the state of having remained in heaven

42 **We now debate** Satan has been careful to establish the basis for his own leadership in these opening remarks, before he even considers what future action should be taken

50 **recked** cared (as in 'reckless'). Moloch's whole speech is based on this characteristic: he would rather suffer any torment than admit his inferiority to God, and can therefore think of nothing but war. Part of the difficulty for Moloch is that he cannot fully know what the extent of torment might be

51 **sentence** opinion

53 **Contrive** plot, use guile. Moloch feels both that he is unskilled in the use of guile and that this is not the time for such subtlety

59 **tyranny** God has now become a tyrant in Moloch's view; in line 64 he uses the word 'torturer'

64 **meet** match, equal

65 **engine** a machine used in war, such as a battering ram or catapult (see, for example, line 923)

69 **Tartarean** hellish (from Tartarus, a place of punishment in the underworld of Greek mythology)

70 **torments** Milton probably intended the specific sense of machines used to hurl stones in addition to the general meaning of 'pains'

74 **that forgetful lake** the 'oblivious pool' of Book I line 266

82 **event** outcome

83 **Our stronger** God

87 **to utter woe** meaning both 'to complete misery' and 'to tell of our misery'

90 **vassals** slaves

97 **essential** essence. Moloch imagines that the worst punishment God could inflict would be to destroy the fallen angels out of existence

99 **if** Moloch cannot know whether or not angels can die

103 **perpetual inroads to alarm** Moloch accepts that victory over God is unlikely. He seeks instead to cause perpetual irritation, through forays into heaven, and thus gain some measure of revenge

106 **denounced** denoted

113 **manna** the food provided by God for the Israelites in the desert

114 **dash** confound

117 **Timorous** fearful

118 **persuasive accent** Belial's principal distinction is the skilfulness of his speech. He can, for example, use irony to emphasise his point (see lines 156–9, where he suggests that God might destroy the fallen angels accidentally or because God has not thought through the consequences)

119 **peers** both 'equals' and 'lords'

124 **he who most excels in fact of arms** Moloch

132 **obscure** hidden

139 **ethereal mould** the substance of heaven

150 **the wide womb of uncreated night** Belial describes the area not yet used for creation as 'night' and as a mother ('womb'). The term 'womb' is further developed later in Book II, in the story of Sin (lines 778 and 798) and the description of Chaos (line 911). Satan addresses the rulers of Chaos as 'spirits of this nethermost abyss, / Chaos and ancient Night' (lines 969–70). There are also references to night in Book I lines 204 and 503, and in Book II lines 439 and 894

156 **Belike** probably

165 **amain** in haste

166 **besought** looked for

173 **intermitted vengeance** vengeance which has been interrupted

175 **stores** storehouses, resources

firmament foundation (usually used of heaven)

176 **cataracts** flood-gates or deluges

177 **Impendent** about to happen

182 **racking** torturing

183 **yon** yonder, over there

188 **dissuades** argues against

189 **him** God

191 **motions** used here in the sense of formal proposals made in a debate, as well as in the more general sense of activities (especially military activities)

216 **inured** grown accustomed. Belial's argument is that the strength of the fallen angels will allow them to survive their current punishment, that they may become accustomed to it, and that God may eventually ease their plight

223–5 **since ... woe** the sense of these lines can be paraphrased as follows: 'our present situation is a poor form of happiness, but not the worst, provided we do not bring further unhappiness upon ourselves'

245 **ambrosial** heavenly

250 **leave obtained** permission given (by God)

263–70 **How oft ... please?** Mammon here compares the state of the fallen angels with that of God hidden in clouds. He argues that God is still as glorious when hidden, and so the fallen angels can create their own glory in the darkness of hell

271 **Wants not** is not lacking in

lustre splendour

275 **our elements** part of our being

278 **sensible** sense, feeling, perception

281 **Compose** come to terms with

285–90 **The assembly ... tempest** an **epic simile** comparing the murmuring of the fallen angels to the sound of wind in rocks at sea

287 **cadence** sound (usually signalling the end of a piece of music)

288 **o'erwatched** weary through keeping watch

bark ship

292 **field** battle

294 **Michaël** the archangel leading the rout of the fallen angels

296 **nether** underworld

297 **policy** cunning statesmanship

310 **Thrones and imperial powers, offspring of heaven** Beëlzebub's opening words echo those of Satan at line 11

312 **style** manner of address

313 **popular vote** vote of the people

327 **iron sceptre** total control. Beëlzebub's line of argument is that, even in hell, the fallen angels will remain under the jurisdiction of God. The matter of whether or not the fallen angels control hell through their occupation of it is one which recurs throughout these opening Books

334 **stripes** from being whipped

336 **to our power** to the fullest extent we can

348 **some new race called Man** in Book I lines 650–4 we were told the rumour of the creation of Eden and the human race

355 **mould** type

357 **attempted** tested

362 **their defence** the defence of Adam and Eve

367 **puny** newly created

374 **Hurled headlong** compare Book I line 45

375 **original** origins

376 **Advise** consider

382 **confound** ruin

384 **Involve** mix

386 **augment** increase: the narrator hints that all will turn out well

391 **Synod** usually a meeting of clergy

397 **Re-enter heaven** Beëlzebub suggests two further reasons for the incursion against mankind: possession of Eden, closer to heaven, may give the fallen angels a base from which to launch a further attack on heaven; and it may prove a more attractive place to dwell than hell

402 **balm** cure, power of healing

406 **palpable obscure** darkness which can be felt

407 **uncouth** unknown

409 **abrupt** abyss

415 **suffrage** selection through a vote

416 **our last hope** Beëlzebub argues as if it were inevitable that a single angel should go on this mission: this is not challenged, but it is not logical. Satan has his own reasons for wanting to travel alone, not least

that he can thereby appear more heroic, because his version of events will
be beyond challenge

423 **Astonished** struck with fear

428 **monarchal pride** the pride of a king; Milton thus compares earthly monarchs
with the hellish Satan

435 **Outrageous** cruel and excessive

immures encloses

436 **adamant** an indestructible material

437 **egress** exit

439 **unessential night** formless darkness

441 **abortive gulf** a gulf which threatens to make the traveller uncreated

442 **scape** escape

448 **public moment** importance to the people

452 **Refusing** if I refuse

457 **intend** ponder

462 **intermit** leave out

470 **erst** formerly

478 **awful** full of respect

481 **general safety** the safety of the majority

484 **specious** unfounded

490 **louring** glowering

497 **men only** only humankind

504 **enow** enough

508 **Midst** in the centre

paramount chief angel

509 **antagonist** enemy

512 **globe** throng

513 **emblazonry** trappings of heraldry

horrent a variant of 'horrid', meaning 'bristling'

517 **sounding alchemy** noisy brass

520 **returned them** answered

Lines 521–628   The description of the fallen angels after Satan's departure

The fallen angels have six distinct occupations: they race, they ride, they
stir up whirlwinds, they sing, they debate philosophy and they explore

their new surroundings. The description of the last group leads the **narrator** to a description of the geography of hell, its four streams and the river Lethe.

The change from the debate to a descriptive section is marked by the inclusion of an **epic simile** (line 533).

The song of the fallen angels (lines 547–50) takes the form of an **epic** poem which celebrates their own heroism: Milton is suggesting that previous epics, which have celebrated military heroism, are inferior in subject to his (see Literary Background on The Epic Tradition).

The description of the philosophical debate held by the fallen angels (lines 558–61) includes the very areas which have most perplexed readers of *Paradise Lost*, especially the relationship between God's foreknowledge and the free will of humanity – see Critical History & Broader Perspectives.

522 **rangèd** drawn up in military order

524 **sad choice** choice causing only sorrow

526 **Truce** respite

    entertain while away

528 **Part** some of them (used likewise at line 531)

    sublime lifted up

530 **Pythian** the Pythian games were held in the ancient Greek city of Delphi every four years

531 **shun the goal** in the game which they are playing, some of the competitors come close to the pole but fail to hit it

532 **fronted** face to face, opposing

536 **Prick forth** advance on horse

    airy belonging to heaven

    couch lower

538 **welkin** sky

539 **Typhoean** giant

    fell horrible

542–6 **As when ... sea** the basis of this simile is an episode from the story of Hercules (Alcides)

543 **envenomed** drenched in poison

547 **Retreated** in seclusion

550–1 **fate ... force ... chance** these terms are employed by the fallen angels throughout the opening Books as ways of accounting for their defeat: they cannot accept the simpler explanation that they were wrong to rebel

552 **partial** meaning 'biased', 'incomplete' and 'sung in different parts'

554 **took with ravishment** enchanted

564 **apathy** calm acceptance

568 **obdurèd** hardened

570 **gross bands** large troops

572 **clime** climate

575 **four infernal rivers** four rivers of hell. Milton's descriptions are based upon the four rivers of Hades, the Greek underworld, and use their Greek names

583 **Lethe** the river of oblivion is, in mythological terms, a more significant river than the other four, and merits a more substantial description

592 **Serbonian bog** according to tradition, Lake Serbonis, in Egypt, was bounded by quicksand which had swallowed armies

594 **parching** drying

595 **frore** frozen; 'Burns frore' is an **oxymoron**

597 **revolutions** periods of time

600 **starve** die of cold – one of the last occasions when the word is used in this more general sense and not to mean specifically death through lack of food. This early meaning is, however, still preserved in some dialects of northern England

601 **pine** suffer pain

604 **sound** stretch of water

611 **Medusa** one of the three Gorgons, whose hair consisted of serpents. The Gorgons were three sisters in Greek mythology whose looks turned to stone anyone who looked at them

613 **wight** creature

614 **Tantalus** a king in Greek mythology who was punished by being placed in a lake of water which receded whenever he tried to drink

619 **dolorous** painful

627 **fables yet have feigned** Milton argues that previous epics have dealt with untrue ('feigned') fables; his material, by contrast, is true

628 **Hydras and Chimeras** monsters of Greek mythology

LINES 629–1055   **Satan's voyage and his encounters, especially with Sin and Death**

As Satan arrives at the utmost bounds of hell, he meets two monstrous creatures who are identified as Sin and Death. He then moves on to meet the figure of Chaos and to come within sight of earth.

> Milton introduces us in this section to two formidable shapes, as yet unnamed. We are to learn in line 760 that one is Sin, and, in line 787, that the other is Death. We have been told (at the beginning of Book I) that the poem would describe how death and woe came into the world; but we have not been led to expect that these would be represented through allegorical **personifications**.

> Milton's technique here owes much to that of the poet Edmund Spenser (?1552–99), whose unfinished work *The Faerie Queene* was the first **epic** poem in English (see also Literary Background). Spenser's description of Error in Book I of his poem is, like Milton's Sin, half woman and half monster, and she is also pestered by a monstrous brood. A more significant connection, however, is that Spenser very frequently introduces figures to his poem which remain unnamed for many lines, just as Milton does here.

633 **scours** moves quickly through

636–43 **As when ... fiend** another epic simile, based upon sea voyages

636 **descried** caught sight of

637 **equinoctial** equally by day and night

642 **Ply stemming** make headway against the wind

645 **thrice threefold** see line 436

648 **unconsumed** see Book I line 69

655 **Cerberean** Cerberus was the monstrous many-headed dog guarding the entrance to hell in classical mythology

656 **list** wished

658 **kennel** live (like dogs in a kennel)

660 **Scylla** one of two mythological monsters (the other being Charybdis) guarding the straits of Messina

662 **night-hag** Hecate, queen of witchcraft in Greek mythology

672 **dart** spear

673 **kingly crown** just as Satan had exhibited 'monarchal pride' (line 428), so here Death wears a kingly crown. Milton contrives to make every reference of kingship evil

677 **The undaunted fiend** Satan

678 **Admired** wondered

683 **athwart** across

686 **Retire** move back

687 **Hell-born, not to contend with spirits of heaven** Satan claims superiority over Death, whom he assumes to be a creature of hell rather than a fallen angel, like himself

693 **Conjured** joined together

696 **reckon'st** compares. Death challenges the claim that Satan is a spirit of heaven

702 **lingering** delaying

709 **Ophiucus** a constellation

710 **hair** the Greek word for comet (line 708) literally means 'hairy star'

724 **snaky sorceress** Sin

728 **thy only son** the revelation that Death is Satan's son comes as a surprise to the reader and to Satan. Their relationship is, in part, a **parody** of that between God and the Son, partly a parody of Eve's creation from Adam's side, and partly an **allusion** to the Greek myth of the birth of Athena

735 **hellish pest** Death ('pest' was a more forceful term in Milton's time than it is now)

736 **Forbore** ceased

738 **sudden** impetuous

739 **Prevented** forestalled

741 **double-formed** i.e. half woman, half serpent

761 **Portentous** exciting admiration

765-6 **such joy thou took'st / With me in secret** if Satan is the father of Sin (line 727), there must be a question as to whether their sexual liaison constitutes incest. This matter is not raised in the case of Adam and Eve, because he is never referred to as her father. What is very clear is that the sexual relationship between Sin and Death is both incestuous and a rape (lines 792–4)

767 **Meanwhile war arose** Homer's epic poem the *Odyssey* recounts Odysseus's adventures and his return home ten years after the fall of Troy. It may be that the reference to the separation of Sin and Satan is intended to remind

the reader of the separation of Penelope and her husband Odysseus in
Homer's poem: Odysseus went to fight an earthly war, whilst Satan went
to fight a war in heaven

768 **fields** wars

771 **empyrean** heavens

772 **pitch** height

780 **Prodigious** both enormous and monstrous

798 **list** wish

800 **repast** food

801 **vex** cause pain (stronger than the modern use of the word)

803 **in opposition** facing one another

808 **bane** poison

814 **he who reigns above** God

815 **lore** lesson

818 **my fair son** a supreme piece of Satanic irony: the ugly Death is anything
but 'fair'

819 **dalliance** sexual pleasure

827 **uncouth errand** mission of which the outcome is unknown

829 **unfounded deep** depths as yet unmeasured

831 **concurring** to the same effect
ere before

832 **round** thoroughly and perfectly formed

833 **purlieus** outskirts

834 **supply** fill up

835 **vacant room** the space left behind by our absence
more removed further away. Satan's logic leads him to conjecture that
humanity has been situated in a new place, rather than in heaven, in case
the population should increase and rebel

837 **broils** disputes

842 **buxom** unresisting

847 **maw** stomach

859 **office** employment, service

864 **author** origin. Eve uses this same word in addressing Adam in
Book IV line 635

869 **voluptuous** giving pleasure

877 **wards** parts of a lock

883 **Erebus** hell

900 **embryon** undeveloped

904 **Barca ... Cyrene** cities in north Africa

910 **Chance** having hitherto been referred to in abstract, Chance is now **personified**, as are Rumour, Tumult, Confusion and Discord at lines 965–7

919 **frith** firth, a narrow inlet of the sea

927 **vans** front wings

933 **pennons** wings

935 **chance** see note to lines 550–1

939 **Syrtis** sandbank

943 **griffin** a legendary creature who guarded gold, which the Arimaspians (one-eyed monsters) attempted to steal (line 945)

964 **Orcus and Ades** two names for the god of hell

965 **Demogorgon** another classical god of hell

980 **profound** depth

982 **behoof** advantage

988 **the anarch old** Chaos

992 **Made head** revolted

1011 **sea should find a shore** Milton's descriptions throughout these first two Books emphasise the differences between stable and unstable locations – see Themes on Uncertainty & Instability

1012 **alacrity** liveliness

1016 **Environed** encircled

1017 **Argo** the ship sailed by the classical hero Jason

1018 **Bosporus** the straits of Constantinople

1019 **Ulysses** the Roman name for Odysseus, one of the principal classical heroes. He is the central character in Homer's epic *Odyssey*
larboard left side

1024 **amain** at full speed

1030 **this frail world** Earth

1042 **Wafts** sails
dubious wavering

1052 **pendent** hanging. The narrative itself becomes pendent at this point, as the focus moves, in Books III and IV, to heaven

1055 **Accursed ... a cursed** a pun: Satan is damned ('Accursed') and the time when he encounters Eden is the hour of damnation ('a cursed hour')
hies hastens

PART THREE

CRITICAL APPROACHES

LANGUAGE & STYLE

The language of *Paradise Lost* has provoked much criticism (see also Critical History & Broader Perspectives). There has been a widespread misconception that John Milton's language is 'difficult', and that he wrote with a syntax and a diction closer to Latin than to English. This has taken a long time to die out, even though it has, in part, been challenged by statistical surveys of Milton's language which have compared his usage with that of other writers. However, these surveys can provide only a limited insight into Milton's practice in his poetry, where it is impossible to discriminate between a strangeness of word order arising from the imitation of another language, and the kinds of inversion which are a necessary consequence of the decision to write in verse.

The following lyric, for example, from Shakespeare's *As You Like It* (II.5.1–8), illustrates some of the ways in which conventional word order changes in the transformation from prose to verse:

Under the greenwood tree
Who loves to lie with me,
And turn his merry note
Unto the sweet bird's throat,
Come hither, come hither, come hither:
Here shall he see
No enemy
But winter and rough weather.

There is a considerable difference between the ordering of the words in this lyric and that in a prose passage expressing the same idea. Yet no critic has suggested that Shakespeare was wrenching the English language; nor has anyone complained of the strangeness of the word order in the following passage from *Macbeth* (II.2.61–3), despite the fact that it includes 'incarnadine', a verb of Shakespeare's own invention, based upon a Latin root: 'this my hand will rather / The multitudinous seas incarnadine, / Making the green one red.' We accept that 'incarnadine' has been separated from 'will' for reasons of emphasis and metre, and that 'the green' probably means 'the green sea'. Detractors of Milton's style have too rarely exercised such acceptance.

It would be possible to attempt a statistical survey of certain features of Milton's poetic style which were felt to be unnatural to the English language, and to compare the incidence of these features in the work of a number of writers. Yet such a survey would probably prove little. Some instances of disrupted word order will seem particularly successful, as in the cases from Shakespeare cited above, whereas a different example of precisely the same disruption will seem discordant. Furthermore, it may not be possible in every case to state with certainty whether or not 'normal' or 'conventional' word order has been followed by Milton. For example, Satan's speech at the beginning of Book II includes the following (lines 14–16):

> From this descent
> Celestial virtues rising will appear
> More glorious and more dread than from no fall

If we were looking for examples of adjectives following nouns rather than, as is usual, preceding them, we might feel that this passage yielded no evidence: it seems quite conventional in its use of adjectives. However, it is at least arguable that the first eight words in this passage could be read either as 'from this fall, heavenly angels will appear rising', as 'from this fall, rising celestial virtues will appear', or as 'from this celestial fall, rising angels will appear'. The lines can thus be read to include two instances of the inversion of adjective and noun, one instance, or none at all.

What may not be sufficiently appreciated, in all the emphasis on Milton's Latinate diction, is his use of graphic English words. For example, in the description of the creation of gold in Book I (lines 700–7), he employs some evocative terms which are all the more effective because they have been part of the English language for a long time, words such as 'dross', 'scummed' and 'sluiced'.

Milton exercises great care in his selection of language, frequently exploiting opportunities for multiple meaning. For example, in Book I lines 713–14, he describes an architectural feature as 'Built like a temple, where pilasters round / Were set'. This seems an odd expression, given that pilasters are rectangular, and yet what Milton is doing is drawing the reader's attention to this apparent **paradox** (line 713), and then resolving it in the line that follows (line 714), by extending the sentence so that it is read to mean 'like a temple, where pilasters were set round'. Similar instances of ambiguity are discussed in the Summaries & Commentaries in relation to 'utter woe' (Book II line 87), 'cope' (Book I line 345) and 'partial' (Book II line 552). We might also note that he uses 'upsent' (Book I line 541) in one of the first recorded instances of the word, and, in contrast, that he is among the last writers to use these particular meanings for 'starve' (Book II line 600) and 'supply' (Book II line 834).

It is difficult not to be impressed by the range of Milton's vocabulary, especially as it relates to the range of his particular fields of knowledge – he is able to draw on detailed technical terms from architecture, from the sea and sailing, and from mining and foundry. Moreover, he reveals a detailed knowledge of the Bible and the Book of Common Prayer, not just in the biblical narratives he **alludes** to, but also in ways of phrasing. For example, the line which is almost Satan's motto – 'Better to reign in hell than serve in heaven' (Book I line 263) – is, in its phrasing, drawn from one of the Psalms which Milton translated in his youth (see Gordon Campbell, *John Milton, Complete English Poems, Of Education, Areopagitica*, p. 156); and the words of Sin to Satan (Book II lines 868–70) are a direct **parody** of the words of the Creed.

Paradise Lost is renowned for Milton's use of the **epic simile**, but it is possible to exaggerate its frequency. There are more epic similes in Book I than in Book II, even though the latter Book is longer. This is because Book I includes more description and fewer speeches than Book II, and this particular stylistic feature is more frequently associated with description. What is impressive about Milton's epic similes is the range of **tenors** he uses, drawn from the Bible (e.g. Book I line 338), from classical legend (e.g. Book I line 197), and from his own contemporary experience (Book I line 287).

USE OF BIBLICAL REFERENCES

The Bible presents the story of the beginnings of all things, a story which precedes all the stories contained in classical legends and classical **epics**.

Milton relies heavily upon the Bible as a source and so it is unsurprising that we should find a wealth of biblical references in his poem. However, Milton also deploys these references in order to make a point about the status of the story which he is telling.

Milton makes no attempt to suppress the notion that large numbers of angels fell with Satan (this is particularly the case in Book I). The catalogue of named fallen angels is extensive, and is followed by a description of the throng of unnamed angels. However, Milton diminishes the effect of all these numbers by undermining their status, comparing them to a swarm of insects (Book I lines 767–92).

In Book I (from line 305 onwards) Milton refers to the story of the parting of the Red Sea. This story, from the book of Exodus, comes near the beginning of the narrative of the escape of the chosen people of Israel to the promised land. However, Milton does not simply refer to this biblical story as part of his **epic simile** – he deliberately mixes it with the more conventional, classical references to Vallombrosa and Etruria. He allots two and a half lines to the comparison with classical epic and ten lines to the reference to the biblical story. A few lines later, Milton refers to the plague of locusts, again from Exodus. Both of these biblical references emphasise the power of God, and God's ability to rescue his believers in circumstances which appear hopeless. Perhaps more significantly, they assert the supremacy of a Christian God over the gods of classical legend.

Thus, when Milton lists the ranks of fallen gods in Book I (line 381 onwards), he begins with those gods whose names are found in the Old Testament. Only after this list does he move on to the gods of classical legend. The intention is clear: to make the material of classical legend and classical epic seem subsidiary to the greater material of Milton's biblically-derived epic.

IMAGES OF THE SUN

Hell is frequently described in terms of **images** of the sea and of night (see also Uncertainty & Instability below). On three occasions in the opening two Books, Milton employs a contrasting image, that of the sun shrouded by clouds. The first is as a **simile** for Satan's appearance (Book I lines 594–9):

> as when the sun new risen
> Looks through the horizontal misty air
> Shorn of his beams, or from behind the moon,
> In dim eclipse, disastrous twilight sheds
> On half the nations, and with fear of change
> Perplexes monarchs.

Here, at a relatively early point in the epic, Milton is making the point that Satan, whilst retaining some remnants of his former glory and light, has now, through his fall, become darkened like an eclipse, and become potentially fearful.

The second, similar simile occurs as part of Mammon's speech, urging the fallen angels not to fear hell (Book II lines 263–70):

> How oft amidst
> Thick clouds and dark doth heaven's all-ruling sire
> Choose to reside, his glory unobscured,
> And with the majesty of darkness round
> Covers his throne, from whence deep thunders roar,
> Mustering their rage, and heaven resembles hell?
> As he our darkness, cannot we his light
> Imitate when we please?

This clever piece of false logic suggests that the rebel angels, now cast into darkness, might regain their former light, just as the sun, if hidden by cloud, does not become permanently darkened.

The third image of sun and cloud is a description of the atmosphere which follows the debate in hell (Book II lines 488–95):

> As, when from mountain tops the dusky clouds
> Ascending, while the north wind sleeps, o'erspread
> Heaven's cheerful face, the louring element
> Scowls o'er the darkened landscape snow or shower,
> If chance the radiant sun, with farewell sweet,
> Extend his evening beam, the fields revive,
> The birds their notes renew, and bleating herds
> Attest their joy, that hill and valley rings.

Here the implication is that the false optimism generated by the debate gives the same illusion of revival to the fallen angels as does a single ray of the sun peeping through the clouds.

These three versions of a single common image serve to draw attention to the great divide which now exists between the place occupied by the fallen angels – a realm of uncertainty, darkness and unpredictability – and the natural world of sun, cloud, evening and morning. In our world we know that clouds will pass and that the night will give way to the morning. For the rebel angels, such certainty has gone.

THEMES

GOD & THE ROLE OF THE NARRATOR

Milton suggests at the outset of his poem that the theme for his **epic** as a whole is to 'justify the ways of God to men' (Book I line 26). In the first two Books of the poem he can accomplish only part of this aim, and, by beginning the action in hell rather than in heaven, Milton has made a deliberate choice of focus, one which conditions the way the reader receives and evaluates the presentation of God.

We learn of God in two ways in the opening books: through what is said about him by Satan and the other characters, and through the comments of the **narrator**. Though God does not appear directly, the reader is constantly aware of God's presence and of his influence on the characters to whom we are introduced.

Apart from the narrator, all those who speak in the opening two Books see themselves as victims of God's power. Chief among these are Satan and the angels who have rebelled and fallen with him, but, at the end of Book II, we encounter Sin and Death, two further characters whose very existence is a direct result of the rebellion against God.

In these circumstances, we are unlikely to receive unbiased views of God from those who speak about him. Milton therefore allows the fallen angels to reveal themselves and their true natures through the ways in which they describe God. For example, Satan's early negative descriptions of God are based on no evidence whatsoever, merely on speculation. He claims in Book I lines 123–4 that God is at that very moment triumphant and joyful over the defeat of the rebel angels, and, a few lines later, that God is vengeful (line 148). Satan has no basis for these claims, any more than he has for using any negative terms (e.g. 'the angry victor', Book I line 169) to describe God or God's motives.

Nevertheless, so skilful is Milton's portrayal of the fallen angels that a grudging acknowledgement of the power of God lurks beneath their words. One early example of this can be found in Book I line 144, where Beëlzebub acknowledges that God must indeed be almighty if he could defeat such a mighty force as that of the rebel angels.

In the face of all these negative views of God, the voice of the narrator has a vital role to play. That voice is not simply there to set the scene at the beginning of Book I or just to give voice to the passages of description found in both of the opening Books. It is there to redress the balance of opinions about God, and to remind readers quietly and with subtlety that everything which takes place within the poem happens solely through the permission of God. Two good examples of the power of this subdued narrative voice can be found in Book I, at lines 211–20 and lines 366–75.

UNCERTAINTY & INSTABILITY

Milton exercises his imagination, and that of his readers, by attempting to describe the very beginnings of time and place. As his poem opens, the first ever event, the war in heaven, has only just taken place, and the characters described by Milton have simply no idea what might happen next, nor what the qualities might be of the environment in which they now find themselves.

The action of these opening Books takes place within a context of uncertainty, and this is represented in two principal forms. On the one hand, the physical spaces described, hell and the regions of Chaos and Night through which Satan travels, are of uncertain character, and the fallen angels are represented as being unclear about the limits and nature of these regions. On the other hand, the rebel angels are also unclear about their own nature. They are aware that they are not as they were before their fall, but they are uncertain about the extent and the implications of this change.

The physical environment in these first two Books is frequently described in terms of **images** of sea and night. For example, in Book I, Satan urges Beëlzebub to seek a 'dreary plain' (lines 180, 183–6):

> Thither let us tend
> From off the tossing of these fiery waves;
> There rest, if any rest can harbour there

Hell is not simply a place of fire, it is a place which lacks the stability of solid ground, and lacks the security of sunlight. These are appropriate images for uncertainty: even today, we know far less about what is in the sea than about the land, and we feel less safe travelling in the dark than by day. In the seventeenth century the sea must have seemed a very challenging environment indeed.

In one of the first extended images of the poem, that of the Leviathan or whale (beginning at Book I line 201), Milton describes Satan in terms of the duplicity and uncertainty of the sea. The vastness of the Leviathan misleads the sailors, lost at night, into thinking that they have found the security of an island. In reality, they have found only a whale.

At the close of Book II, Satan encounters the forces of darkness and Chaos, and this entire passage is couched in terms of **metaphors** of the sea. The gates which Sin lets open reveal 'The secrets of the hoary deep – a dark / Illimitable ocean without bound' (Book II lines 891–2).

Satan, having come to terms with this environment, is described as 'glad that now his sea should find a shore' (Book II line 1011) and, as he comes to the edge of Chaos, Satan finds himself 'like a weather-beaten vessel' which 'holds / Gladly the port, though shrouds and tackle torn' (Book II lines 1043–4).

THE PRESENTATION OF SATAN

The principal character introduced in these opening Books is that of Satan. He is the first figure we meet, and he is presented as the leader of the rebel angels who find themselves in hell. In particular, Satan seeks to find some point of stability and security in this new and uncertain environment. He looks within himself for the source of this stability, referring to his 'fixed mind' (Book I line 97) and his 'mind not to be changed' (Book I line 253). However, like the other angels who find themselves in hell after their rebellion, the extent of Satan's real unfixedness of mind is revealed in the first word he speaks. His opening speech begins 'If', and the fallen angels wrestle throughout these opening Books with their lack of knowledge about what the future might bring: again and again they ask 'what if' (for example, Book I line 143).

Satan attempts to use his considerable powers of imagination and oratory to change the environment of hell, and to make what is clearly monstrous and terrifying appear acceptable and even desirable. Early in the opening Book he declares that 'The mind is its own place, and in itself / Can make a heaven of hell, a hell of heaven' (Book I lines 254–5). This audacious claim to an ability to use language to alter reality is, in a sense, an extension of Satan's most notable attribute, his powers of **rhetoric** and flattery.

For much of the opening two Books of *Paradise Lost* Satan's speeches are public rather than private. We see him speaking to rally his troops in Book I and participating in formal debate and boasting of his prowess in Book II. Only rarely are we given a glimpse of his real sense of pain, for example in Book I lines 54–6:

> the thought
> Both of lost happiness and lasting pain
> Torments him

Certainly this inner torment is never revealed to his peers. His speeches are thus designed to persuade and to flatter.

His initial approach to the fallen angels begins by reminding them of the titles which they formerly enjoyed: 'Princes, potentates, / Warriors, the flower of heaven' (Book I lines 315–6); and he is still addressing them by these titles in Book II: 'Powers and dominions, deities of heaven' (line 11).

He flatters Beëlzebub in a parallel fashion (Book I lines 85–7):

> him, who in the happy realms of light,
> Clothed with transcendent brightness, didst outshine
> Myriads

To Satan it seems that the method most likely to rouse his fallen peers is to remind them of how great they once were. To some extent, the description of Belial at the beginning of Book II (lines 110–17) replicates some of the qualities of satanic flattery and exposes its falseness.

Perhaps the most ironic instance of Satan's flattery, and the example which best illustrates its hollowness, comes at the end of Book II, in his meeting with Sin and Death. His initial reaction to these hideous monsters is: 'nor ever saw till now / Sight more detestable than him and thee' (Book II lines 744–5). Yet when he has finally realised who these creatures are and what their relationship to him is, his mode of address changes to 'Dear daughter' and 'my fair son' (lines 817 and 818).

Satan exercises a fascination for readers partly because his is the first voice we hear (see Satan & Drama below), but also because he seems to have certain characteristics which we readily identify as 'human'. For example, in Book I line 118, Satan speaks of having learned from experience, and of profiting from that experience in future actions. We are very accustomed to this process in our own lives, but we may easily fail to see that Satan's experience and his capacity to learn from it is intimately linked with his fallen state. Satan seems to be like us because he demonstrates aspects of being fallen, as humans do.

Satan & Drama

There has been considerable critical interest in the figure of Satan in *Paradise Lost*, and in the possibility that he may be the true **hero** of the **epic** (see also Critical History & Broader Perspectives). Milton's nephew, Edward Phillips, asserted that it was Milton's original intention to write a tragic drama on the subject of the fall (see Note on the Text). The attractiveness of Satan and the genesis of *Paradise Lost* as a drama are to some extent interwoven. It is a critical commonplace that, in drama, the audience is led to sympathise with and believe in the first voice they hear, especially if that voice speaks directly to the audience. In his book *Engagement with Knavery* (Duke University Press, Durham, 1986) R.C. Jones demonstrates how this principle operates in Renaissance plays such as Shakespeare's *Richard III*. One reason why there is any case for regarding Satan as the hero of the poem is that we learn his version of events first and, by the end of Book II, we have received only this partial account of the war in heaven.

One characteristic of Satan which is particularly evident in the opening two Books of *Paradise Lost* is his desire to rouse his fallen troops; to do this, he may well need to paint for them a more positive picture of what they have just experienced than is strictly true. S.A.J. Bradley, in the introduction to his translation of *Genesis B* (see Note on the Text), says of the relationship between *Genesis B* and *Paradise Lost*: 'Both poets, as a direct consequence of opting for an epic heroic genre, risk counterproductively investing the rebel angel with an admirable dignity and heroic appeal which are inherent in the traditional diction and manner of the genre' (*Anglo-Saxon Poetry*, Everyman, 1982, p. 12). We should note Bradley's reference here to the 'opting', that is, making a choice: it is all too easy to forget that *Paradise Lost* is the product of much deliberate choice on Milton's part. Bradley goes on to compare the presentation of Satan in both poems with that of the Anglo-Saxon hero, Beowulf, and of Byrhtnoth, hero of the *Battle of Maldon*. One feature of the latter is that Byrhtnoth is defiant in the face of what seems to be certain defeat, and this defiance gives rise to a stirring turn of speech. For example (from Bradley's prose translation in *Anglo-Saxon Poetry*, p. 521):

> Do you hear, sea-wanderer, what this nation says? They will give you spears as tribute, the poison-tipped javelin and ancient swords, those warlike accoutrements which will profit you nothing in battle. Seamen's spokesman, report back again; tell your people much more distasteful news: that here stands a worthy earl with his troop of men who is willing to defend this his ancestral home, the country of Aethelraed, my lord's nation and land. The heathens shall perish in battle. It seems to me too despicable that you should take to your ships with our riches, unfought, now that you have intruded this far hither into our country. Not so smoothly shall you get gold. First point and edge shall sort things out between us, the fierce exchange of fighting, before we pay tribute.

This kind of expression is known as **flyting**. It is found frequently in Anglo-Saxon poetry and is also a characteristic of the style of the Elizabethan dramatist Christopher Marlowe, who deployed **blank verse** with great expertise in many of his plays. Satan's defiant words to Death in Book II of *Paradise Lost* can be described as an instance of flyting.

Drama, especially that of Marlowe and of his contemporary Shakespeare, operates through an interchange of dialogue and **soliloquy**, public scenes and private scenes. In Books I and II of *Paradise Lost*, all the scenes are public, and we find no instance of a soliloquy, which is often more revealing of the true feelings of a character than the dialogue. However, Satan does have later soliloquies which do much to undercut whatever initial impression we may have formed of his valour.

It would be wrong to place too much emphasis on the dramatic qualities of *Paradise Lost*, because it is a poem, despite its dramatic origins. However, there is one aspect of the difference between drama and epic poetry which readers must be aware of, and that is the difference between reading a poem and watching a play.

When watching a play, the members of the audience must receive and interpret what is happening at a single sitting. They cannot interrupt the action and ask for explanation or for difficult scenes to be replayed. Thus, if the meaning of a particular word is obscure, the audience will have to ignore it, forget it, or hope that the general context will carry them through to understanding. In reading, however, there is a real danger that any word which has an obscure meaning will cause readers to stop and to turn for help outside the text. This may well have the unfortunate effect of making the text seem more difficult than it really is, and it will almost certainly inhibit the flow of the narrative. It is therefore important that readers of *Paradise Lost* try very hard to keep reading, perhaps noting words which are not clear in meaning, but not interrupting their reading to look them up immediately.

There is another difference between drama and a written text which merits consideration. Most dramas tell their narratives entirely through the interchange between characters, and relatively few employ the device of the **narrator**. However, in *Paradise Lost*, as in many other written texts, the narrator plays a crucial role both in moving the story onward and in shaping the reactions of the readers. This is particularly the case in Books I and II, where the only characters we meet are the fallen angels Sin, Death and Chaos. In these circumstances we might be in danger of being in total sympathy with the forces of evil, were it not for the narrator, who intervenes, for example, to point out the vanity and falseness of what is being said in the debate at the beginning of Book II. Indeed, so significant is this narrative voice that we may need to reflect upon whether Satan's really is the first voice we hear in the poem, or whether we have already learned to attend to the narrator before Satan speaks for the first time.

PART FOUR

Textual Analysis

TEXT 1   (BOOK I LINES 44–83)

This passage comes shortly after the very beginning of the poem. It introduces us to the power of God and to the nature of hell.

> Him the almighty power
> Hurled headlong flaming from the ethereal sky
> With hideous ruin and combustion, down
> To bottomless perdition, there to dwell
> In adamantine chains and penal fire,
> Who durst defy the omnipotent to arms.
> Nine times the space that measures day and night
> To mortal men, he with his horrid crew
> Lay vanquished, rolling in the fiery gulf,
> Confounded, though immortal: but his doom
> Reserved him to more wrath; for now the thought
> Both of lost happiness and lasting pain
> Torments him; round he throws his baleful eyes,
> That witnessed huge affliction and dismay,
> Mixed with obdurate pride and steadfast hate;
> At once, as far as angels ken, he views
> The dismal situation waste and wild:
> A dungeon horrible, on all sides round,
> As one great furnace flamed, yet from those flames
> No light, but rather darkness visible
> Served only to discover sights of woe,
> Regions of sorrow, doleful shades, where peace
> And rest can never dwell, hope never comes
> That comes to all, but torture without end
> Still urges, and a fiery deluge, fed
> With ever-burning sulphur unconsumed:
> Such place eternal justice had prepared
> For those rebellious; here their prison ordained

In utter darkness, and their portion set,
As far removed from God and light of heaven
As from the centre thrice to the utmost pole.
O how unlike the place from whence they fell!
There the companions of his fall, o'erwhelmed
With floods and whirlwinds of tempestuous fire,
He soon discerns; and weltering by his side,
One next himself in power, and next in crime,
Long after known in Palestine, and named
Beëlzebub. To whom the arch-enemy,
And thence in heaven called Satan, with bold words
Breaking the horrid silence, thus began

The process of naming is highlighted in this extract. There are three named participants here: God, Satan and Beëlzebub, although the company of fallen angels is also mentioned, referred to as 'his horrid crew' and 'the companions of his fall'. We learn from lines 80–2 that, while Satan has already received his name, Beëlzebub will acquire his name much later in Palestine: Milton attempts to make his poem encompass all of history. The power of God, and of God's control, is immediately emphasised. It is that power which dominates the entire **epic**.

Almost all of the epic, and certainly all of its first two Books, takes place before time began, yet the poet needs to find a mechanism for describing the passage of time. He does so here, for example, by referring to the time it took for the fall to take place as 'Nine times the space that measures day and night / To mortal men'. By including reference to 'mortal men' and by referring to human history in the naming of Beëlzebub, Milton makes us part of the action of his poem.

The poem operates by moving between heaven, hell and Eden and by emphasising the differences between these three distinct regions. This section is dominated by the description of the pain of hell, contrasted with two brief references to heaven, as 'the ethereal sky' and as 'the place from whence they fell'. The poem also consistently deals in extremes and superlatives: everything about the regions which it describes is incomparable. Throughout, Milton uses terms such as 'bottomless', 'omnipotent', 'ever-burning', 'unconsumed', 'utter' and 'utmost'.

The passage demonstrates the care which readers must employ in coming to *Paradise Lost*. On the one hand, the overall meaning of the passage should be clear enough, even on the first reading; on the other hand, more careful examination will reveal the great subtlety of Milton's writing. For example, a modern-day reader may be surprised by the use of 'utter' as a term expressing extremes. In Milton's time 'utter' meant 'outer', just as 'utmost' signified 'outermost'. Similarly, the term 'horrid' is not nowadays a particularly powerful word, but in Milton's day it could carry the sense of 'terrifying' or 'revolting'.

Milton is famous – perhaps even notorious – for the scope of his **allusions**, both biblical and classical. Some readers will find this reputation daunting, but this extract demonstrates very clearly that we do not have to possess Milton's breadth of knowledge to appreciate *Paradise Lost*. There are at least two classical allusions in this passage: one, in the nine days of the fall, to the fall of the Titans in Hesiod's ancient Greek *Theogony*; the other, in the reference to the absence of hope, to Dante's fourteenth-century *Inferno*. However, readers who do not immediately recognise these allusions are not prevented from understanding the meaning of the passage.

One of the most notable features of this extract is a classic instance of the literary figure called the **oxymoron**: 'yet from those flames / No light, but rather darkness visible' (lines 62–3). 'Darkness visible' is a **paradox**: darkness cannot be seen. Yet Milton's use of this paradox is a powerful and graphic description of the extent of the darkness in hell, so terrible and palpable as to seem visible. William Golding was sufficiently struck by this oxymoron to use it as the title for his 1979 novel; twenty-five years earlier he had taken the translation of 'Beëlzebub' (which derives from Hebrew) as the title for his first novel, *Lord of the Flies*.

The whole of *Paradise Lost* is written in **blank verse**. When blank verse is used at its most straightforward, each line takes the form of a single sentence. At the very beginning of this extract, however, far from having each sentence bound by a single line, Milton begins a new sentence in the middle of a line and runs it on into the next. Moreover, in order to add a greater sense of cohesion between the different parts of the sentence, he includes **alliteration**, which he continues across three lines: 'Him', 'Hurled', 'headlong' and 'hideous'. As a further example of this play between syntax and metre, Milton seems almost to be ready to bring the sentence to a close towards the end of line 46, only to use the final syllable of the line to begin a new phrase: 'down / To bottomless perdition'. Just as the sense of the passage is of an endless process of fall, so this bold use of the metre reinforces that motion being perpetually renewed.

There is a particular kind of thematic contrast in the middle of this extract, where Milton places 'peace' and 'rest' on the one hand and 'torture without end' on the other. This is a significant distinction, not least because much of literature is concerned with the glorification of movement and ambition, giving little credit to peace and stillness. *Paradise Lost*, however, seeks to emphasise the negative aspects of change, especially the folly of seeking to change what is perfect. The urging of endless torture in this extract is mirrored by the reaction of Satan to Eve and Adam in Book IV (lines 509–11). There, he recognises that what they experience is love, while his fate is to have:

> neither joy nor love, but fierce desire,
> Among our other torments not the least,
> Still unfulfilled, with pain of longing pines

The dominant **metaphor** of this extract is that of the sea voyage. Satan and his companions, his 'crew', have been 'rolling in the fiery gulf', and are now 'o'erwhelmed / With floods and whirlwinds'; Beëlzebub himself is 'weltering' (one of Milton's favourite words). The subtlety of this metaphor has not always been fully appreciated, because we tend to think of hell simply as a lower region. This metaphor of the voyage emphasises not only the pain of the process of the fall, but also the idea that the fallen angels are condemned never to find a stable landing place. Even in hell they continue to be overwhelmed and to welter.

TEXT 2   (BOOK I LINES 752–98)

This passage, from the end of Book I, describes the assembling of the council of fallen angels in Pandemonium. It exemplifies the descriptive power of the narrative, and the way in which the voice of the **narrator** operates.

Meanwhile the wingèd heralds, by command
Of sovereign power, with awful ceremony
And trumpet's sound, throughout the host proclaim
A solemn council forthwith to be held
At Pandemonium, the high capital
Of Satan and his peers; their summons called
From every band and squarèd regiment
By place or choice the worthiest; they anon
With hundreds and with thousands trooping came
Attended; all access was thronged; the gates
And porches wide, but chief the spacious hall
(Though like a covered field, where champions bold
Wont ride in armed, and at the soldan's chair
Defied the best of paynim chivalry
To mortal combat, or career with lance),
Thick swarmed, both on the ground and in the air,
Brushed with the hiss of rustling wings. As bees
In spring-time, when the sun with Taurus rides,
Pour forth their populous youth about the hive
In clusters; they among fresh dews and flowers
Fly to and fro, or on the smoothèd plank,
The suburb of their straw-built citadel;
New rubbed with balm, expatiate, and confer
Their state-affairs: so thick the airy crowd
Swarmed and were straitened; till, the signal given
Behold a wonder! They but now who seemed
In bigness to surpass Earth's giant sons
Now less than smallest dwarfs, in narrow room
Throng numberless – like that pygmean race
Beyond the Indian mount, or fairy elves,
Whose midnight revels, by a forest side
Or fountain, some belated peasant sees,
Or dreams he sees, while overhead the moon
Sits arbitress, and nearer to the earth
Wheels her pale course: they, on their mirth and dance
Intent, with jocund music charm his ear;
At once with joy and fear his heart rebounds.

Thus incorporeal spirits to smallest forms
Reduced their shapes immense, and were at large,
Though without number still amidst the hall
Of that infernal court. But far within,
And in their own dimensions like themselves,
The great seraphic lords and cherubim
In close recess and secret conclave sat,
A thousand demi-gods on golden seats,
Frequent and full. After short silence then,
And summons read, the great consult began.

When we describe the dramatic qualities of *Paradise Lost*, and try to define those features which make it seem like a play (see Critical Approaches on Satan & Drama), we must not lose sight of the role of the narrator. The narrator has two distinct roles in *Paradise Lost*: first, to supply the descriptions which are so vital to the progress of the poem; second, to influence our sympathies and to manipulate our responses to the text. In this extract, the narrator, whom we may broadly accept as being Milton himself, is acting out both roles. He is describing the setting-up of the council, whilst at the same time ensuring that we are not deluded by its apparent magnificence.

In the space between Text 1 above (lines 44–83) and this passage from the end of the first Book, there has been a significant narrative development. The fallen angels are no longer 'weltering' in an unstable environment – they have obtained some measure of stability and established a court. However, this apparent move to civilisation cannot be taken at face value, as the narrator is at pains to point out. This is the first example in history of the establishing of a court, and it is founded by the fallen angels: the very evident implication is that it, and all subsequent courts, are wicked and to be scorned. This may thus be a reference to the political situation of Milton's own time (see Background).

The passage exemplifies Milton's powers of linguistic innovation, in that it includes a word now in common usage, which Milton invented specifically for this poem. A situation in which there is a large amount of chaos and noise is today often described as 'pandemonium', a word which first occurs in this extract, and which Milton coined (by combining Greek word forms) to refer to the place of all demons.

The passage also includes what is a rarity in *Paradise Lost*, a humorous pun. At line 790, Milton uses the expression 'at large' in two different senses. On the one hand, this means simply 'free to move about', in the sense that an escaped criminal might be described as 'at large'; on the other hand, 'at large' is in ironic contrast to what has happened in the narrative. In order to enter Pandemonium, the fallen angels are forced to reduce their size to their 'smallest forms', and yet are still 'at large'.

TEXT 3   (BOOK II LINES 430–73)

This extract largely takes the form of a speech, by Satan. It is a relatively straightforward passage, certainly no more difficult to comprehend than many speeches from plays by Shakespeare. (For further discussion of the perceived difficulty of Milton's language, see Critical Approaches on Language & Style.)

> 'O progeny of heaven, empyreal thrones;
> With reason hath deep silence and demur
> Seized us, though undismayed; long is the way
> And hard, that out of hell leads up to light;
> Our prison strong, this huge convex of fire,
> Outrageous to devour, immures us round
> Ninefold; and gates of burning adamant,
> Barred over us, prohibit all egress.
> These passed, if any pass, the void profound
> Of unessential night receives him next,
> Wide gaping, and with utter loss of being
> Threatens him, plunged in that abortive gulf.
> If thence he scape, into whatever world,
> Or unknown region, what remains him less
> Than unknown dangers, and as hard escape?
> But I should ill became this throne, O peers,
> And this imperial sovereignty, adorned
> With splendour, armed with power, if aught proposed
> And judged of public moment in the shape
> Of difficulty or danger, could deter

Me from attempting. Wherefore do I assume
These royalties, and not refuse to reign,
Refusing to accept as great a share
Of hazard as of honour, due alike
To him who reigns, and so much to him due
Of hazard more, as he above the rest
High honoured sits? Go therefore mighty powers,
Terror of heaven, though fallen; intend at home,
While here shall be our home, what best may ease
The present misery, and render hell
More tolerable; if there be cure or charm
To respite or deceive, or slack the pain
Of this ill mansion: intermit no watch
Against a wakeful foe, while I abroad
Through all the coasts of dark destruction seek
Deliverance for us all; this enterprise
None shall partake with me.' Thus saying, rose
The monarch, and prevented all reply;
Prudent lest, from his resolution raised,
Others among the chief might offer now
(Certain to be refused) what erst they feared,
And so refused might in opinion stand
His rivals, winning cheap the high repute
Which he through hazard huge must earn.

This is a stirring piece of **rhetoric**, the flaws of which are apparent only after careful re-reading and reflection. On first acquaintance, the reader is likely to be impressed by the speech, and it is only after the voice of the **narrator** intervenes at line 466, to reveal Satan's anxiety about others volunteering, that we are sent back to revise our initial views. Milton is extremely skilful in luring his readers into finding Satan admirable.

The passage is very revealing of the character of Satan, and of the tactics he employs to maintain control over his fallen troops. The speech begins by emphasising the difficulty of the task of tempting mankind, by detailing the terrors of leaving hell. Yet this is spurious, for Satan is actually volunteering to mount an escape, and we learn from the final lines of the passage, after the speech has ended, that Satan is anxious to ensure that he alone is able to embark upon this journey.

Another tactic which Satan employs is to flatter his troops. They are not, as far as he is concerned, fallen angels, but rather 'progeny of heaven' and 'empyreal thrones' (line 430). This is a device he employs later in Book II when he encounters Death (line 687). If the fallen angels are 'peers' (in the sense of both 'equals' and 'lords'), then Satan's leadership of them makes him all the more exalted.

PART FIVE

BACKGROUND

HISTORICAL BACKGROUND

John Milton lived through one of the most turbulent periods of British history, a time which included the trial and execution of a monarch, and the ruling of the country by someone with no claim to the throne: these are both unique events. When Milton was born, in 1608, James I had been on the throne of England for five years. After the death of Elizabeth I, James, as the first monarch of the House of Stuart, united the thrones of England and Scotland, but he proved to be very unpopular with Parliament and with many of his people.

Believing that he had been called to rule by God's command rather than by the will of the people or the consent of their representatives, James clashed frequently and violently with Parliament over the control of the country's government, and particularly its finances. King James also thought that he should control the Church through its bishops; but a group of people, increasing in numbers and strength as the years went by, objected to the power of those bishops and to corruption in the established Church. These men, the Puritans, realised that abuses (such as one priest holding more than one living) were being retained, and resented the fact that the authority of the Pope had been replaced by that of the King as head of the English Church. The Puritans strove for a purer and more austere form of worship and Church organisation. Thus the two forces of Puritanism and Parliamentarianism together resisted the absolutism of the monarchy, at first by constitutional means, seeking reform of abuses, and then, from 1642 onwards, by force of arms.

The son of James I, Charles I, quarrelled bitterly with Parliament from his accession in 1625 until 1629, when he tried to rule without a Parliament at all. This was neither illegal nor unconstitutional, because the King had every right to call Parliament as it suited him. A Scots invasion forced Charles to recall Parliament in 1640 to vote for funds for an army, but he disagreed with them once again, only to find his chief minister, the Earl of Strafford, and his Archbishop of Canterbury,

William Laud, removed from office and executed. Finally, in 1642, the
King took up arms to crush the forces of Parliament in civil war.

Although successful in the early stages of the war, Charles faced a
powerful combination in the alliance of Parliament with the Scots, the
loyalty of London to the parliamentary cause, and the brilliant military
leadership of Oliver Cromwell. As Charles's fortunes declined, he was
beaten in decisive battles at Marston Moor in 1644 and Naseby in 1645.
He surrendered, and was imprisoned, tried, condemned and beheaded in
1649. Thereafter Cromwell ruled as Lord Protector until his death in
1658; but the Commonwealth became increasingly unpopular, and there
was no strong character to succeed Cromwell. So, in 1660, the royal
House of Stuart was restored to the English throne in the person of
Charles II (Charles I's son), a man of questionable morals but of
considerable political astuteness. When John Milton died in 1674,
Charles II had been on the throne for fourteen years. A further fourteen
years were to pass before a second revolution, this time relatively
bloodless, continued the process of securing parliamentary control in
England and fashioning a constitutional monarchy.

MILTON'S LIFE

John Milton, born in London in 1608, believed himself to be a divinely
inspired writer. From his youth onwards he considered himself capable of
employing that gift in a magnificent and celebratory work. Although the
epic which he eventually wrote declares itself to be concerned with the
disobedience, and hence the folly, of mankind, it also predicts the
restoration of mankind through the sacrifice of the Son, and can thus
claim to incorporate a subject which is both tragic and majestic.

No other English poets have been as closely involved in the political
events of their time as Milton was. He was a national figure, not only
supporting the Republican cause of Oliver Cromwell, but also working
for Cromwell during the period of the Protectorate (see Historical
Background above). Ironically, the man who has the best claim to be
regarded as England's finest poet (Shakespeare's reputation rests largely
on his plays) was better known to his contemporaries for his prose
pamphlets than for his poems. Moreover, because of the controversial

opinions which he expressed in those pamphlets, Milton was the subject of scathing comments from a number of other writers.

In consequence, we know a great deal about what Milton's contemporaries thought of him and, because Milton was ready to defend himself from attack, we have a considerable body of writing in which Milton describes himself, his life and his aspirations. For example, his 1654 pamphlet *The Second Defence of the People of England*, originally written and published in Latin, is, in large part, a defence of himself in answer to a detractor. Milton gives us in that pamphlet this account of his early life (cited from *Milton's Prose Writings*, ed. K.M. Burton, Everyman, 1974, pp. 341–2):

> My father destined me from a child to the pursuits of literature; and my appetite for knowledge was so voracious, that, from twelve years of age, I hardly ever left my studies, or went to bed before midnight. This primarily led to my loss of sight. My eyes were naturally weak, and I was subject to frequent headaches; which, however, could not chill the ardour of my curiosity or retard the progress of my improvement. My father had me daily instructed in the grammar-school, and by other masters at home. He then, after I had acquired a proficiency in various languages, and had made a considerable progress in philosophy, sent me to the University of Cambridge. Here I passed seven years in the usual course of instruction and study, with the approbation of the good, and without any stain upon my character, till I took the degree of Master of Arts.
>
> After this I did not, as this miscreant feigns, run away into Italy, but of my own accord retired to my father's house, whither I was accompanied by the regrets of most of the fellows of the college, who showed me no common marks of friendship and esteem. On my father's estate, where he had determined to pass the remainder of his days, I enjoyed an interval of uninterrupted leisure, which I entirely devoted to the perusal of the Greek and Latin classics; though I occasionally visited the metropolis, either for the sake of purchasing books, or of learning something new in mathematics or in music, in which I, at that time, found a source of pleasure and amusement. In this manner I spent five years till my mother's death.

There is every reason to believe that this passage, although written in response to particular attacks, gives an accurate account of Milton's early life and his aspirations. He was born into a family who could afford to pay for a good quality of education for their son. He attended university, where his attractive appearance was commented upon, and where he may have quarrelled with his tutor, and certainly found the syllabus and the conversation little to his taste.

Milton's love of solitude and of self-directed study is evident in the autobiographical passage cited above, and his life was characterised by self-discipline and individualism. As far as we can gather, he made few close friends, and the one person to whom he was most attached in his youth, Charles Diodati, a school friend, died in 1638. That death and the drowning of one of Milton's fellow students, Edward King, whom Milton knew much less well than he did Diodati, caused the poet to spend time considering the brevity of life, in elegies in Latin and in English. Indeed, Milton's early poetic output is characterised by the variety of languages he is able to employ. The greatest poet in the English language had no little facility in Italian, Latin and Greek.

After Cambridge, Milton did not train for a profession, as his brother Christopher did, nor did he enter the Church: instead, he set about pursuing his own reading at his father's estate, Horton in Buckinghamshire. He enjoyed some success as a writer during this period, producing a masque in 1634, later published under the title *Comus*. In 1638 Milton began an extensive European tour, and it is to this event that he refers in the extract above. His detractors had claimed that Milton, aware of the increasingly difficult political situation in England, had decided to abandon his country and 'flee' to the safety of continental Europe. Milton disputes this. He cut short his tour because of the situation in England, but did not hurry unduly on his way home. Nor did he join the armies of the Parliament on his return, but devoted himself instead to the education of his two nephews, the Phillips brothers, and to the composition of pamphlets which attacked the excesses of the Bishops and supported the Presbyterians.

The years 1642–3 mark the end of what might be called Milton's first period, and the beginning of his second. From a personal point of view, his prolonged education was complete. Poetically, he had already written his early lyric poems: the 'Nativity Ode'; *L'Allegro* ('the happy man') and the companion *Il Penseroso* ('the serious man'); the masque *Comus*; the pastoral elegy *Lycidas*; and a number of sonnets, among them the autobiographical 'Twenty-Third Birthday'. Moreover, his experience as a pamphleteer had taught him, even at this early stage, that his enemies would seek to discredit his ideas by attacking his own personal behaviour.

The second period of Milton's life was one of public office and political pamphleteering, with a few sonnets the only poetry he produced. After his return from his European tour, Milton had involved himself in the political controversies of the day by writing pamphlets against the Bishops. In 1642 he married Mary Powell, the daughter of a Royalist household in Oxford with which his father had had business dealings; indeed, despite Mary's obvious physical attraction for Milton, this was primarily a marriage by arrangement, and was certainly no love match on her side.

It appears that Mary quickly found the Puritan austerity and intellectual stature of her husband too much for her, and returned home. The war made reclamation difficult. Many commentators would claim that it was his own bitter personal experience which led Milton to justify divorce by reference to scripture in four pamphlets. Others point out that Milton had grounds for divorce under the existing laws, that his pamphlets, if accepted, would have given women rights in the settlement of divorce much more extensive than those proposed by any of his contemporaries, and that Milton never did in fact divorce Mary.

The pamphlets on divorce were condemned by Presbyterian theologians, who were already, in 1643, severely limiting the licensing of books. Milton believed that two of his most strongly held principles were endangered: the right of individual interpretation of scripture, and his freedom of speech and writing. So, in 1644, he published *Areopagitica*, his most celebrated pamphlet, inspired by love of liberty and devoid of the usual personal scurrility. His sympathies were now with Cromwell and the army section of the Parliamentarians with their greater religious tolerance, rather than with the Presbyterians. In 1649 Milton was appointed Latin Secretary to the Commonwealth with the official title of Secretary for the Foreign Tongues: the revolutionary government used Latin as its language of diplomacy, and the learned Milton was a natural choice. His main tasks were to write pamphlets justifying government policy, particularly the execution of the King; to defeat the champions of the Royalist cause on paper; and to compose official despatches to the courts of Europe, from Stockholm to Savoy. The strength of Milton's views against monarchy and against elaborate religious practices can be clearly seen in the early books of *Paradise Lost*, in which he loses no opportunity to portray kings and bishops negatively.

By 1652 Milton had lost his sight completely, and in 1655 he was allowed a substitute Secretary. He now turned his mind back to poetry, although he continued to write anti-monarchical pamphlets until 1660, the year of the Restoration.

Milton's third period was characterised by personal defeat and disillusion, but celebrated in his literary output by his three great poems *Paradise Lost*, *Paradise Regained* and *Samson Agonistes*. This final period coincided approximately with the first fourteen years of the Restoration (1660–74), though there are grounds for believing that he wrote Satan's address to the sun (*Paradise Lost*, Book IV lines 32–113) as early as 1658. At the time of the Restoration, Milton, as a well-known Cromwellian, was in some physical danger, but the Royalist poet Sir William Davenant, placing poetry before politics, concealed him until the danger had passed. From then on, Milton – blind, ailing and impoverished – lived quietly and unpersecuted in the midst of his triumphant enemies, visited by many friends and admirers, until his death in 1674.

LITERARY BACKGROUND

The autobiographical references in Milton's prose, his letters, his Commonplace Book (his private journal), and the **allusions** to other writers throughout his work give an indication of the range of reading which he undertook in his commitment to become a poet. We shall never have a complete list of Milton's reading, but the selection we know of makes the study of his writing, the poetry in particular, a daunting task and scarcely a year goes by without a new source being discovered for one of his works.

From a modern perspective Milton can appear something of a conformist, a reactionary writer. He invented no new poetic forms and, even in his prose, where it might be assumed that there was scope for formal innovation, he adopted traditional **rhetorical** modes whenever possible. However, we should bear in mind not only the particular political circumstances which led Milton to present himself as a respectable, establishment figure writing within an accepted tradition, but also the fact that Milton left none of these traditional modes untouched by his own originality. The **epic**, the tragedy, the masque, the pastoral elegy and the sonnet were all shaped by Milton to fresh ends, and concepts such as heroism, victory and defeat were redefined.

For Milton, traditions were there to be used, rather than to prescribe behaviour. He undertook rigorous personal preparation in becoming a writer, having found the syllabus at Cambridge deficient for his needs. After preparing himself for a life as a priest, he found that the practices of the conventional Church were abhorrent to him and thus devoted himself to training as a poet, only to find that events forced him to join the pamphleteering war. However, Milton saw no grave inconsistency between priesthood, poetry and prose writing. There was little fundamental distinction for him between prose and poetry, and indeed some passages from his prose read with the fervour and inspiration of poetry:

> Then, amidst the hymns and hallelujahs of saints, some one may perhaps be heard
> offering at high strains in new and lofty measure to sing and celebrate thy divine
> mercies and marvellous judgement in this land throughout all ages.

In the passage above, from *Of Reformation* (1641), Milton is writing of the development of England as a nation and of his role as poet in celebrating that triumphal movement towards reformation. In his early Latin poem to his father, 'Ad Patrem', Milton catalogues the attributes and magnificences of poetry. Poetry was, for Milton, not only part of the educational curriculum for the cultured man, it was also a product of that education. Thus poetry did not represent a retreat from the issues of the world into pretty fancies, but an engagement with them and an attempt to mould minds and opinions through the power of words.

In *The Reason of Church Government* (1641) Milton sets out his views on the roles of poet and priest, and on the differences between good and bad poets. He says, of the gifts of poetry:

> These abilities ... are the inspired gift of God, rarely bestowed, but yet to some
> (though most abuse) in every nation; and are of power, beside the office of a
> pulpit, to inbreed and cherish in a great people the seeds of virtue and public
> civility, to allay the perturbations of the mind, and set the affections in right

tune … to deplore the general relapses of kingdoms and states from justice and God's true worship.

The poet, therefore, ranks equally with the priest as an instructor. Milton seems to feel rather as his near-contemporary George Herbert (1593–1633) does in 'The Church Porch':

> A verse may find him, who a sermon flies,
> And turn delight into a sacrifice.

Good poetry is to be distinguished from bad poetry not on the grounds of technical deficiency (although it may be distinct in that respect too), but on the grounds of its moral content, as Milton explains in *The Reason of Church Government*:

> the writings of libidinous and ignorant poetasters; who, having scarce ever heard of that which is the main consistence of a true poem … do for the most part lay up vicious principles in sweet pills to be swallowed down, and make the taste of virtuous documents harsh and sour.

This view is evident in Milton's earliest poetry. In *Lycidas* the virtuous and worthy characters are associated with the music of true, moral poetry: 'Who would not sing for Lycidas? He knew / Himself to sing, and build the lofty rhyme' (lines 10–11); and harmony is equally associated with virtue in *Comus*, *L'Allegro* and *Il Penseroso*.

As Milton explains in *An Apology for Smectymnuus* (1642):

> he who would not be frustrate of his hope to write well hereafter in laudable things, ought himself to be a true poem; that is, a composition and pattern of the best and honourablest things; not presuming to sing high praises of heroic men, or famous cities, unless he have in himself the experience and practice of all that is praiseworthy.

Throughout his career, Milton is careful to present himself as a 'true poem', a virtuous man whose views are therefore worth listening to, and to attack the views of his opponents because they are not 'true poems'. For Milton, the validity of an argument depended upon the integrity of the person who advanced it, and to teach this lesson was one of the functions of poetry. In this respect he was following in the direct line of writers such as Philip Sidney (1554–86) and Edmund Spenser (?1552–99), both of whom emphasised that the educational aspect of poetry was more important than its power to entertain. Milton was a great admirer of Spenser, whom he mentions in *Areopagitica* (1644) as 'our sage and serious poet'. Indeed, Milton's first volume of collected verse, *Poems 1645*, was advertised as an imitation of Spenser.

Spenser's declared aim, as stated in the preface to his epic *The Faerie Queene*, seems close to that of Milton: 'The generall end therefore of all the books is to fashion a gentleman or noble person in vertuous and gentle discipline.' Spenser, however, was able to do this without risking giving offence to those in power; Milton had to take much greater risks to convey his educational message.

Milton did not have to follow in the line of Sidney and Spenser. He could have done as George Herbert did before him and Andrew Marvell was to do after him; he could have written in the metaphysical style of John Donne. This witty, detached manner of writing was available for the expression of personal, political or religious ideas, but Milton chose not to adopt it. The cultural theorist Raymond Williams has characterised the difference between Milton's position and that of the metaphysical poets. Milton, he suggests, temporarily suspended what is usually called literature, but did not suspend his writing, during a brief period of conflict. The metaphysical poets, by contrast, found 'a way of holding divergent attitudes towards struggle or towards experience together in the mind at the same time' (cited by B. Sharratt, 'The Appropriation of Milton', *Essays and Studies* XXXV, 1982, p. 30). These, Williams argues, are two legitimate possibilities for any highly conscious person in a period of crisis.

By the time the political crisis was at its height, Donne and Herbert were dead; but in any case, the poems which they wrote describing their crisis of faith were very different both in character and in function from Milton's religious poems. They were private expressions of their individual relationships with their God, sometimes uncertain, often passionate. They are striking and dramatic and, in the case of Herbert, often deceptively simple. In neither case was Donne or Herbert writing for a public platform and, indeed, neither found a publisher for his religious verse in his own lifetime.

Milton, on the other hand, felt that the situation of the moment demanded either celebration or explanation, and was far less concerned with his own relationship with God than with the larger issues of determining what God's will for God's people might be. It is ironic that Milton should be associated in the popular mind with egoism, when there is far less self-interest in his poetry than in that of many of his contemporaries. (Such views may well derive from Robert Graves's 1942 novel *Wife to Mr Milton*.) Some of Milton's characters may express doubts (Satan, in particular) about the ways of God, and there may be shifts, and even inconsistencies, in Milton's views from work to work, but each individual poem or prose pamphlet attempts to convince its readers of Milton's own absolute certainty on theological issues.

When in 1649, for example, the point at issue is whether a king has a relationship with God different from that of his subjects, Milton delivers his opinion confidently: 'all men naturally were born free, being the image and resemblance of God himself, and were, by privilege above all the creatures, born to command, and not to obey' (*The Tenure of Kings and Magistrates*).

However, Milton showed on one occasion that he could in fact also write in the manner of Herbert if he chose; he could investigate his own faith more personally. The sonnet 'When I consider how my light is spent', which he left unpublished for over twenty years, provides an intimate insight into Milton's private uncertainties and the way in which he resolved them.

THE EPIC TRADITION

In order to fully appreciate Milton's achievement in *Paradise Lost*, it is necessary to have an understanding of the **epic** tradition in which he casts his poem, and of the position which he believed *Paradise Lost* to occupy within that tradition.

In Book II we are introduced to an example of the composition of an epic within *Paradise Lost* itself. In the description of the way the fallen angels occupy themselves after Satan has departed, we find that the fourth group of angels chooses to compose an epic (lines 547–50):

> sing
> With notes angelical to many a harp
> Their own heroic deeds, and hapless fall
> By doom of battle

The fallen angels' epic seems designed to portray a false and flattering view of their history – their actions are hardly 'heroic', and their fall in battle is anything but 'hapless'. This connection between epic and history, to which Milton draws our attention, is a key to the understanding of the epic tradition.

Two writers of very different temperaments have provided similar statements on the relationship between epic and history. Samuel Johnson wrote, in *The Lives of the Most Eminent English Poets* (1783), that an epic:

> relates some great event in the most affecting manner. History must supply the writer with the rudiments of narration, which he must improve and exalt by a nobler art, animate by dramatic energy and diversify, by retrospection and anticipation.

The American poet Ezra Pound put the same idea more succinctly in 1961: 'An epic is a poem including history' (cited by P. Merchant in *The Epic*, Methuen, 1971, p. 1). The notion of this link between epic form and historical content is one which has persisted from the beginnings of the genre through to the current use of the term 'epic' in popular prose: a novel (or film) such as *Gone with the Wind* or *East of Eden* will be labelled 'epic', not merely because of its length but because it embraces a wide sweep of history and because its central characters are to be regarded somehow as representative of a particular stratum of society. Even when the term is used of a sporting encounter – a soccer match which remains unresolved after two replays, or a fifteen-round heavyweight boxing contest – it is not length alone which leads to this usage, but the suggestion that this event has been memorable enough to merit a place in the folk-mythology of the town or country of which the protagonists are representative.

By tradition, epics are long narrative poems, majestic both in theme and style. They deal with legendary or historical events of national or universal significance, involving action of broad sweep and grandeur. Moreover, most epics deal with the exploits of a single representative individual, thereby giving unity to the composition. There is thus usually no confusion as to who is the **hero** of the epic. Often, an epic involves the introduction of supernatural forces that shape the action, conflict in the form of battles or other physical combat, and certain stylistic conventions: an invocation to the Muse, a formal statement of the theme, long lists of the protagonists involved, and set speeches couched in elevated language. All of these conventions are in evidence in *Paradise Lost*.

The poet Alexander Pope (1688–1744), writing a **parody** of a definition of an epic in the style of a cooking recipe, neatly summarised its essentials (cited by P. Merchant in *The Epic*, Methuen, 1971, p. 64):

> Take out of any old Poem, History-books, Romances, or Legend ... those Parts of Story which afford most Scope for long Descriptions ... Then take a Hero, whom you may chuse for the Sound of his Name, and put him into the midst of these Adventures: There let him *work*, for twelve Books; *For the Moral and Allegory.* These you may Extract out of the Fable afterwards at your Leisure: Be sure you strain them sufficiently.

Throughout *Paradise Lost*, however, Milton constantly dismisses the kind of epic based upon historical adventure. Such poetry has become, for Milton, mere 'fable', a term which he tends to employ pejoratively. Milton has chosen not to follow the example of European poets like Luís de Camões (1524–80) who, in *Os Luciados*, celebrated the history of the Portuguese people. Neither does he imitate Edmund Spenser's *The Faerie Queene*, a **panegyric** for the England of Elizabeth I. Milton is employing poetry in his epic not to celebrate history but to explain it and, at times, to suggest that the interpretation of recent events by his contemporaries was flawed.

In part, however, Milton's reasons for selecting a subject for his poem which was not drawn from English history would be similar to those of Abraham Cowley, who wrote in the preface to his own epic on the life of David (1656):

> It is not without grief and indignation that I behold that *Divine Science (Poesie)* employing all her inexhaustible riches ... in the wicked and beggerly *Flattery* of great persons.

The traditional epic implied an association between the aspirations of the poet and that of the nation the poet was celebrating and, as in the case of *The Faerie Queene*, could hardly avoid some measure of flattery of the head of that nation. Milton could not, therefore, compose a traditional epic after the failure of his hopes for a revolution (see Milton's Life): the English nation of the Restoration was not a possible subject for his celebration, and thus his epic sets out to denigrate the traditional

preoccupations of nationhood and individual achievement. Having
described the fallen angels writing a false epic in Book II, Milton returns,
towards the end of *Paradise Lost*, to question the traditional subjects of
the epic (Book XI lines 689–97):

> in those days might only shall be admired,
> And valour and heroic virtue called;
> To overcome in battle, and subdue
> Nations, and bring home Spoils with infinite
> Manslaughter, shall be held the highest pitch
> Of human glory …
> Destroyer rightlier called and plagues of men.

This is a radical redefinition of the central concern of traditional epics,
the victory in battle of one race over another: such battles are, in Milton's
terms, manslaughter and destruction, and therefore do not constitute true
heroism.

Thus Milton's epic differs from that of Spenser not simply because
it comes later in time, and is therefore able to build upon it; nor even
because Milton was a better poet than Spenser (although few would
dispute that he is). It differs because the social and historical changes
which had occurred between Spenser's time and that of Milton made it
impossible for Milton to develop the epic within the conventional
nationalistic tradition of which Spenser was a part.

Epic poems were not intended merely to be entertaining stories of
legendary or historical heroes; their role was to summarise and express the
nature or ideals of an entire nation at a significant or crucial period of its
history – this is the function of the ancient Greek epics the *Iliad* and the
Odyssey, for example. Thus the characteristics of the hero of a traditional
epic are likely to be national rather than individual traits, and the exercise
of those traits in heroic deeds serves to gratify a sense of national pride.

The conventional epic is inherently retrospective, rehearsing the
earlier triumphs of a nation in order to reassure its present citizens – just
as Satan tries to rouse the fallen angels at the beginning of *Paradise Lost*
by telling them stories of their 'glorious past'. Milton has therefore
changed this perspective drastically by setting out to go beyond the task
of merely explaining how things came to be the way they are, and
suggesting instead that the history has not yet been completed, and that

things may yet change. *Paradise Lost* describes the continuing failure of humanity, the blindness of the majority, and celebrates the providence of God, a providence which has yet to be totally realised.

By electing not to describe the triumphs of humanity up to a particular point in past history, and instead implying that there is no fixed point, the Restoration of the monarchy can be accounted for and accommodated within Milton's scheme as a purely temporary phenomenon, a further instance of the error of the majority. *Paradise Lost* implies that the error of Restoration will eventually be reversed; but that reversal, like the redemption of humanity by the Son, lies outside the scope of the history of the poem.

The decision to treat history in this manner has a direct effect on the narrative perspective. History in *Paradise Lost* is either distorted or telescoped and startling effects are produced, such as the combination of epic and pastoral conventions when Satan reaches Eden. Milton's pastoral setting is not, as it might have been conventionally, on the periphery of the poem, a place of temporary solace for a battle-weary warrior: it is the central location of the poem, and the place to which we all must aspire. One result of this means of treating history is that it is virtually impossible to read the narrative line of *Paradise Lost* as if it had a beginning, a middle and an end, as, for example, William Empson's interpretation (see Critical History & Broader Perspectives) would imply.

The 'partial' song of the fallen angels in Book II lines 547–50 seems, if detached from its context, the stuff of conventional epic, and Milton leaves readers at this stage of the poem to draw their own conclusions about the morality of the angels' satanic epic. It becomes clear, however, from Raphael's account of the war in heaven much later in the poem (Books V and VI), that the battle was far from glorious, and that it was, if anything, somewhat ridiculous and pointless: in the fallen angels' epic Satan is a hero, whereas the true history shows him to have been vain and self-absorbed. One lesson to be drawn might be that Milton intended his readers to equate the satanic view of history with that of the Royalists, and to decide that the apparent victory of the Restoration would eventually be proved to have been an illusion.

Paradise Lost is a great poem, but it is also a disappointing poem, and quite deliberately and consistently so. Just as Satan's invention of a glorious past is frustrated by the reality of the war in heaven, and his ambition of victory over mankind gives way to the anticlimax of deception by an apple (an irony which even Satan finds amusing), so the reader's expectations and hopes are continually frustrated by a poem which denies glory to activity and substitutes instead the primacy of obedience, an attribute which includes being obedient enough to do nothing if the need for inaction should arise. Milton is continually asserting the futility of action throughout the poem. The crisis of the world is not going to be resolved by a single, gloriously flamboyant military victory, any more than the issues of the civil war in England were settled at battles such as Naseby or Worcester. The conventional epic, however, reassures its readers with just that fiction: it operates through a narrative in which military heroism on the part of a minority can overcome evil for the majority, who abdicate their problems to the conventional hero. The majority will be happy to abdicate responsibility for their fate in this way, and conventional epic reinforces this willingness by rewarding its readers with stories of heroes who will fight on their behalf. *Paradise Lost* does not do this: nobody secures victory for the readers, and they are left only with the promise that Christ will one day return to win a victory for all.

THE ENGLISH EPIC

Paradise Lost is written in English, and yet one of the two commendatory poems published in the 1674 edition (see Note on the Text), that by Samuel Barrow, was written in Latin. At this point in time, English had not yet fully supplanted Latin as a language capable of being used for the most serious subjects. Milton himself wrote Latin and Greek poetry as well as poetry in English, and, in the period when he worked for Cromwell's administration (see Milton's Life above), his prose documents were composed in Latin too. In the Renaissance it was becoming increasingly the case that European nations were seeking to advance the status of their own vernacular languages, and one form of promoting them came through having an epic composed in that tongue.

Edmund Spenser had begun the process of securing for England its first epic in English, in his uncompleted poem *The Faerie Queene*, but Barrow recognised that Milton's achievement was greater, both in terms of its subject matter and in that it was written in this country (Spenser was writing in Ireland): 'Who that has hoped for this would believe that it would ever be written? And yet the land of Britain reads these things today' (Gordon Campbell, ed., *John Milton, Complete English Poems, Of Education, Areopagitica*, 1990, p. 145).

There had in fact been an epic in English even before Spenser: the Anglo-Saxon period produced the magnificent poem *Beowulf*. However, the manuscript of that early poem was undiscovered and inaccessible in Milton's time and in that era the line of English poetry tended to be traced back only as far as Geoffrey Chaucer (*c.* 1343–1400).

Milton was more interested in his literary relationship with the great classical poets than in a relationship with any English writer, but the descriptions in Book II of Sin and Death and, to a lesser extent, of Chaos, demonstrate his debt to Spenser. Furthermore, alongside the many classical **allusions** (see Summaries & Commentaries), there are also many references in Books I and II to Milton's own contemporary situation in England, especially in his disparaging references to kings and to churches (see above).

PART SIX

CRITICAL HISTORY & BROADER PERSPECTIVES

CRITICAL HISTORY

The critical history of *Paradise Lost* is, unsurprisingly, a history of the reception of the poem as whole and not merely of its opening Books. However, as discussed below, much criticism from the twentieth century has focused on the alleged deficiencies in Milton's presentation of God. It may be, therefore, that the decision of examination boards to concentrate study on Books I, II, IV and IX serves to confirm that temptation is described more vividly than redemption, and that the poem is at its most interesting when not presenting God.

EARLY CRITICISM

The early editions of *Paradise Lost* sold well (particularly in comparison with Milton's first volume of poetry, *Poems 1645*), and Milton received royalty payments for his **epic**. However, it was not until the publication in 1688 (after Milton's death) of a lavish and illustrated subscription edition of the poem that it could be claimed that *Paradise Lost* had achieved the status of an English classic. As the critic W.W. Robson remarked in a 1982 essay (in *The New Pelican Guide to English Literature*, ed. B. Ford, 1982, p. 243):

> In this present age, when it is rarely read except by scholars and literary specialists, we are likely to forget how popular *Paradise Lost* once was. It stood on the shelves of every respectable household, beside the Bible and *The Pilgrim's Progress*.

This very popularity, however, could be said to have worked against the liveliness of Milton's epic. It seems to have led to an unquestioning reverence of the poem on the part of many readers, and to the production of pale imitations of Milton's style by inferior poets, who failed to see that Milton is quite consciously placing himself at the end of a literary tradition. *Paradise Lost*, in many respects, denies the validity of the epic poem (see Literary Background). However, Milton has never at any stage been totally beyond negative criticism, even on the part of his supporters.

The essayist Joseph Addison (1672–1719), for example, wrote a series of papers on Milton for *The Spectator* in 1712 in which he finds the poet 'sublime', and yet this very assertion led Addison to defend and discuss aspects of *Paradise Lost* which he felt failed to live up to this quality. Furthermore, the edition of *Paradise Lost* produced in 1732 by Richard Bentley (1662–1742) went as far as to amend those passages in the poem which the editor did not understand or did not like, on the grounds that these sections could not represent what the poet had intended.

Bentley justified some of his changes by claiming that Milton's original text was too shocking to have been what the poet intended; ironically, he thus emphasised one of the most conspicuous qualities of *Paradise Lost*. Milton undoubtedly intended his poem to shock and to challenge, and however eccentric Bentley's reading of the poem may be, it is arguable that Milton would have preferred Bentley's active engagement with the text to the passive acquiescence which more traditional readers have accorded it. Milton, after all, continually advocated the need for an explicit faith which was constantly renewing itself by challenge and debate, and the presence of recurring Milton controversies over the past two-and-a-half centuries has ensured that successive generations of serious readers have had their faith in Milton's epic enhanced by trial.

EIGHTEENTH-CENTURY VIEWS OF MILTON'S LANGUAGE

The language of *Paradise Lost* has been the subject of debate from Joseph Addison and Samuel Johnson onwards. Addison, as cited in *The Living Milton* (ed. F. Kermode, Routledge, 1960, p. 162) argued that Milton:

> has carried our language to a greater height than any of the English poets have ever done before or after him, and made the sublimity of his style equal to that of his sentiments.

However, he also complained on the very same page that 'our language sunk under him, and was unequal to that greatness of soul which furnished him with such glorious conceptions.' Johnson, more trenchantly, capped Addison's remark with this comment from *The Lives of the Most Eminent English Poets* (1783), claiming that Milton had:

formed his style by a perverse and pedantic principle. He was desirous to use
English words with a foreign idiom … Of him, at last, may be said what Jonson
says of Spenser, that *he wrote no language*.

And of *Paradise Lost* as a whole, he wrote a few pages earlier:

> *Paradise Lost* is one of the books which the reader admires and lays down, and
> forgets to take up again. None ever wished it longer than it is. Its perusal is a duty
> rather than a pleasure.

Echoes of johnson and addison in the twentieth century

There can be a variety of reasons which lead a critic to write negatively of
a poet, and Johnson's attacks owe as much to what he believed of Milton
the man as to his views on poetry. The poet and critic T.S. Eliot
(1888–1965) shared Johnson's antipathy towards Milton the man, and he
was not content simply to accuse Milton of having had a bad effect on
later English poetry. He also claimed in *On Poetry and Poets* (Faber, 1957)
that Milton lacked visual imagination, that his poetry gave priority to
sound rather than to meaning, and that his language was remote (p. 154):

> Every distortion of construction, the foreign idiom, the use of a word in a foreign
> way or with the meaning of the foreign word from which it is derived rather than
> the accepted meaning in English, every idiosyncrasy is a particular act of violence
> which Milton has been the first to commit.

In his second essay on Milton, Eliot shifted ground somewhat. Here
he claimed that this remoteness was a mark of Milton's greatness, but
the recantation was not allowed: the critic F.R. Leavis (1895–1978)
continued the crusade against Milton which Eliot had begun by declaring
that Milton's language was monotonous, pompous, laboured, pedantic
and artificial. His attack in *Revaluation* (Chatto & Windus, 1936) was
uncompromising (p. 53):

> So complete, and so mechanically habitual, is Milton's departure from the English
> order, structure and accentuation that he often produces passages that have to be
> read through several times before one can see how they go, though the Miltonic
> mind has nothing to offer that could justify obscurity – no obscurity was intended:
> it is merely that Milton has forgotten the English language.

Leavis's attack upon Milton's language was based on several false premises. It tended to portray the 'grand style' of Milton's **epic** as unvarying and unwieldy, incapable of subtlety or delicacy, and incomparably poorer than the style of either Shakespeare or Spenser. The effect of the attack has been to prompt the publication of a number of excellent studies of *Paradise Lost*, each of which has demonstrated new intricacies in Milton's handling of the varied style of his epic. There are, undeniably, occasions when the style manifests complexity (a less emotive term than Leavis's 'obscurity'), but these occasions are always when a complex issue is being presented.

As Jonathan Richardson (1665–1745), an early commentator on *Paradise Lost*, observed in *Remarks on Milton's Paradise Lost*, the reader needs to be especially vigilant:

> A Reader of *Milton* must be Always upon Duty; he is Surrounded with Sense,
> it rises in every Line, every Word is to the Purpose ... he Expresses himself So
> Concisely, Employs Words So Sparingly, that whoever will Possess His Ideas
> must Dig for them, and Oftentimes pretty far below the Surface.

Since this remark was made as long ago as 1734, it is odd that critics in the twentieth century should have continued to describe the language of *Paradise Lost* as mere music, as if Milton were using the sound of the words as an alternative for thought. Leavis's version of this line of attack, in *The Common Pursuit* (Chatto, 1952, p. 62), is at least consistent with his other views on Milton: 'the man who uses words in this way has ... no "grasp of ideas", and, whatever he may suppose, is not really interested in the achievement of precise thought of any kind.'

C.S. Lewis (1898–1963), however, writing ostensibly in defence of Milton in *A Preface to Paradise Lost* (Oxford University Press, 1942) against the attacks of Eliot and Leavis, seems to come very close to finding Milton's language mere music himself (p. 23):

> The epic diction, as Goethe said, is 'a language which does your thinking and your
> poetizing for you' ... The conscious artistry of the poet is thus set free to devote
> itself wholly to the large-scale problems – construction, character drawing,
> invention; his *verbal* poetics have become a habit, like grammar and articulation.

The work of later critics such as Christopher Ricks, Stanley Fish and others has demonstrated convincingly that Milton's epic diction is far from being a substitute for thought, and that it was no more subject to habit than his grammar or his use of metre. Although Milton employs impressive catalogues in his epic, these are not simply there to be magnificent. The scholarship of recent editors has indicated the extent to which Milton carefully constructs these catalogues either to undermine the reader's confidence in the character or situation being described, or to challenge the status of earlier epics.

THE DEBATE ON GOD & SATAN

Attacks on John Milton in the twentieth century have been almost exclusively concerned with *Paradise Lost* (some critics wishing that Milton had continued to write as he did in *Lycidas*). They have done great service to the poem by posing questions and provoking responses which might otherwise never have been explicitly and systematically formulated. These attacks, mounted by some of the foremost writers of the century, have centred, oddly enough, on the very issues raised in Samuel Barrow's commendatory verses in the edition of 1674 (see Note on the Text). Barrow's verse, written in Latin and less frequently quoted than that of Andrew Marvell, observes of Satan (in Gordon Campbell's translation): 'What a Lucifer ... hardly inferior to Michael himself!'; and it asks why any reader should read *Paradise Lost* without reading it in its entirety. These are, in effect, the main preoccupations of twentieth-century criticism of *Paradise Lost*: whether the reader can be expected to enjoy the entire poem, and whether Satan is presented too attractively.

Interest in the presentation of God and Satan in *Paradise Lost* is no new phenomenon, but it has proved a lively area of recent Milton study, in an age when **epic** language and epic conventions are unrecognised, and faith in God and a knowledge of the Bible cannot be taken for granted. The modern reader provides the ideal test for the validity of *Paradise Lost*.

Following William Blake's remark at the end of the eighteenth century in *The Marriage of Heaven and Hell* that 'The reason Milton wrote in fetters when he wrote of Angels & God, and at liberty when of Devils & Hell, is because he was a true Poet and of the Devil's party without knowing it', the character of Satan began to exercise a considerable influence on English fiction, especially through the villains of Gothic novels, who are often recognisable as Satan in all but name. A whole range of fictional characters with satanic qualities can be found in novels from Charlotte Brontë's *Jane Eyre* (1847) and Emily Brontë's *Wuthering Heights* (1847) to William Faulkner's *Light in August* (1932). The influence of *Paradise Lost* is particularly notable in Mary Shelley's *Frankenstein* (1818), in which the monster reads Milton's poem and finds in it the explanation of its problem (Everyman edition, 1963, pp. 135–6):

> I often referred the several situations, as their similarity struck me to my own. Like Adam, I was apparently united by no link to any other being in existence; but his state was far different from mine in every other respect. He had come forth from the hands of God a perfect creature, happy and prosperous, guarded by the especial care of his Creator ... but I was wretched, helpless, and alone. Many times I considered Satan as the fitter emblem of my condition; for often, like him, when I viewed the bliss of my protectors, the bitter gall of envy rose within me.

In many respects Mary Shelley's novel is tantamount to a reinterpretation of *Paradise Lost*. Her attempt to translate her reading of Milton's epic into the medium of the Gothic novel is as revealing as the heroic opera *The State of Innocence and Fall of Man* (1678), for which Milton gave his permission, by John Dryden (1631–1700).

For further discussion of Milton's influence on the Romantic view of Satan, see K. Gross, 'Satan and the Romantic Satan: a notebook' in *Re-Membering Milton* (eds M. Nyquist and M. Ferguson, Methuen, 1987) and, for a more wide-ranging treatment of Milton and Romanticism, Leslie Brisman, *Milton's Poetry of Choice and Its Romantic Heirs* (Cornell University Press, 1973)

WALDOCK'S VIEW

In 1947, the critic A.J.A. Waldock systematised the feeling which had become popular through Gothic interpretations of Milton – that Satan was an attractive figure, ill-deserving of his fate – in his book *Paradise Lost and Its Critics* (Cambridge University Press). Approaching the poem from the perspective of one well-versed in reading novels, Waldock argued that Milton had been so successful in his description of a powerful and attractive Satan in Books I and II of *Paradise Lost* that he had been forced to jettison this character altogether and to replace him with the degraded Satan who appears in the later Books.

If all the books and articles on Milton were burned except those written between 1950 and 1980, future generations might be led to feel that Waldock's critique of *Paradise Lost* had been outstandingly influential, because so many critics have written defences of the poem against Waldock's attacks, far more than have attempted to repudiate Empson's attacks in *Milton's God* (see pp. 87–9 of this Note). The truth is, however, that Waldock's thesis can be overturned relatively easily, whereas Empson's charges are much weightier.

Paradise Lost is neither a novel nor a drama, and Waldock's attention to speeches (or parts of speeches) and incidents fails to do justice to Milton's creation of a poetic narrative. Although ostensibly concerned with the development of the narrative in the poem, Waldock is not above considering incidents in an entirely different order from that in which Milton has placed them, or omitting vital details of their presentation. Writing, for example, of the temptation of Adam by Eve at the end of Book IX, Waldock describes the incident entirely in terms of the speeches made by the two characters, and asks us to judge whether or not Adam should have yielded on the basis of this dialogue. He fails to point out the effect of the context in which this exchange takes place and, in particular, the **symbolism** of the description of Adam's meeting with Eve: he with a garland of flowers which fade as soon as Eve tells her news, she with a bough from the Tree of Knowledge. These details are crucial both to our evaluation of the scene and to Adam's guilt. Similarly, although he censures Milton for intruding authorial comments about Satan which undermine the magnificence of his early speeches, Waldock himself attempts to persuade us by imagining the reaction of the fallen angels to these speeches: Milton chose when to give us these reactions and when to withhold them. Waldock, therefore, provides a critique upon a poem which is not Milton's *Paradise Lost*, and lays charges against Milton which are quite unfair: for Waldock, hell is not described in sufficiently concrete detail, and yet, if it had been, Milton's God would have been truly vengeful and the debate among the fallen angels in Book II would have been utterly pointless – the only possible outcome of being sent to a hell of concrete pain could be the attempt to escape.

RESPONSES FROM BURDEN AND FISH

Principal among the virtues of Waldock's book is the fact that it raised some real questions about what happens in *Paradise Lost* (whether, for example, Eve's fall is of a different order from that of Adam), and that it prompted two detailed defences of *Paradise Lost*: one from Dennis Burden (*The Logical Epic*, Routledge, 1967) and the other from Stanley Fish (*Surprised by Sin*, University of California Press, 1967). Neither of these critics disagrees with Waldock's assertion that Milton portrays Satan attractively. What they claim, however, along with other recent critics of the poem, is that Milton does this quite deliberately and that the anti-epic or satanic epic aspects of *Paradise Lost* are a conscious part of Milton's design.

The Logical Epic takes the reader back to Milton's poem and away from the speculation about issues which may arise from the poem. It may be stimulating to argue about whether God's foreknowledge predetermines the fate of mankind, but it is more relevant for the student of *Paradise Lost* to investigate, as Burden does, how Milton contrives his description of God to make it seem that mankind has free will by, for example, making certain decisions about his description of the fall of Eve and Adam (p. 32):

> In Book IX all is done out of human decision, and the Fall unfolds in a
> series of human problems. God has already foretold it, but his foreknowledge
> is here kept apart from the foretold event and is fulfilled ... without
> comment.

Burden's approach to the poem, like that of Fish, carefully emphasises the choices which Milton has made in the setting-out of his narrative, and discriminates between those parts of the poem which derive from the Bible and those which are of Milton's own invention. As modern readers, we face real difficulties in assessing the success of *Paradise Lost*, partly because our knowledge of the Bible tends to be far less detailed than that of Milton's contemporaries, and we are therefore liable to make a mistaken assessment of Milton's originality; partly because we may have insufficient experience with other epics to be able to recognise anti-epic features in the poem; and partly because we need constantly to remind ourselves that this massive work is the product of human invention – it is not 'given', but came about as a result of a set of choices which Milton made. The work of both Burden and Fish has done much to help the modern reader cope with these problems.

Burden suggests that the poem contains within it a 'satanic epic', of which Satan is the **hero**, and argues convincingly that Satan constantly thinks of himself in terms of the attributes of the hero of a conventional epic: ambitious, courageous and representing his people against the might of a fierce oppressor. This self-portrait extends beyond the early Books in hell, and is part of his method for tempting Eve, in the guise of a serpent (Book IX lines 687–90):

> Look on me,
> Me who have touched and tasted, yet both live,
> And life more perfect have attained than fate
> Meant me, by venturing higher than my lot.

Burden says of these lines: 'Satan is claiming to have acted as the typical hero of his own sort of poetry, a satanic epic about "Their own heroic deeds"'(p. 143). Yet this satanic epic proves to have a disappointing climax for its hero when, as he later reports to hell, he seems to have effected the downfall of mankind not through a great military triumph, but with an apple.

Paradise Lost is quite explicitly a poem intended to educate, as Milton declares at the beginning of its first Book, where he asks for inspiration to 'assert eternal providence, / And justify the ways of God to men' (lines 25–6). Part of the process of education is the rejection of the attractions of the satanic epic, and the exercising of judgement in recognising satanic heroism from its true counterpart. It is at this task that Adam fails, responding to Eve's false epic just as Eve had responded to Satan's: 'Bold deed thou hast presumed, adventurous Eve, / And peril great provoked, who thus hast dared' (Book IX lines 921–2). In *Paradise Lost*, to be daring and adventurous is hardly ever the right course of action.

Stanley Fish's book is a detailed investigation of the process undergone in reading *Paradise Lost* and of the ways in which the reader is tempted by the attractions of the satanic epic. The thesis of the book is substantially in accord with that of Burden, and together these two critics present a lucid case for regarding *Paradise Lost* as a carefully constructed and remarkably innovative work.

Good as their defences are, both Burden and Fish find *Paradise Lost* less than totally successful (they agree that the final two Books provide a challenge for Milton, with less opportunity for innovation). Neither critic completely solves all the puzzles of the poem: it is unlikely that any single reading will ever do this. There are still questions which remain unanswered from Waldock, and from Empson.

William Empson (1906–84) is the author of one of the most provocative books on Milton yet written. *Milton's God* (Chatto & Windus, 1961) draws not only upon Empson's own atheism, but also upon his experience of having lived and taught outside Western Europe. It raises challenging questions about Milton's portrayal of God, some of which have never satisfactorily been answered.

Empson's approach in *Milton's God* differs from that of earlier detractors of Milton, including C.S. Lewis and T.S. Eliot, in that he has read the poem extraordinarily carefully, in order to establish the precise grounds for his dissatisfaction. His attack is in general far more illuminating, and more entertaining, than, for example, C.S. Lewis's *Preface to Paradise Lost*, which is written in support of the poem yet adopts an unchallenging stance towards it. Indeed, Empson is able to point with justification to instances of assertions by Lewis which betray an inaccurate reading of the text. Empson says, of Lewis's view of Mammon (*Milton's God*, p. 53):

> Lewis treats him as a sensualist fighting down his pangs of shame – 'Honour? Love? Everybody I meet salutes me, and there is an excellent brothel round the corner.' But Milton tells us that one of the chief pains of Hell, as in human prisons, was deprivation of sex, if it may be so called.

This may look like an example of pettiness, scoring niggling points against the minor inaccuracies of one's opponent, but Empson's desire for precision of thinking in relation to *Paradise Lost* serves to indicate the fine distinctions being drawn within the poem. Occasionally Empson breaks his own rules and implies that a statement has been made in the poem when it is, in fact, Empson's own invention. Writing, for example, of the account by Beëlzebub of the creation of man, he observes: 'God sounds particularly like Zeus in this devil's account, whereas Raphael reports him later in the poem as saying he is going to create us to spite the devils' (p. 56). Raphael's account, of course, makes no mention of spite as a motive on God's part.

Sometimes Empson distorts the text of the poem so that the opinions expressed by a character are taken to be the equivalent of Milton's own views, ironically making himself guilty of a fault which John Peter, an earlier detractor of Milton, had derided (in *A Critique of Paradise Lost*, Longman, 1960, p. 27):

> to wrench the characters and incidents of *Paradise Lost* from their artistic context, and then to consider them as if they were autonomous ... disregarding the significance which has been conferred on them by the poem.

Commenting on a description of Satan, Empson observes (*Milton's God*, p. 38): 'If he *endangered* the rule of God, the rule of God is not inherently *perpetual*.' Yet the **paradox** of having these two contradictory terms juxtaposed derives not from Milton's muddled thinking but from the mind of the character, Beëlzebub, who delivers the line.

In general, Empson's thesis is rigorously and logically expounded: if God had foreknowledge, and he knew that mankind would fall even before the revolt of Satan, then the whole poem presents God in a very bad light, playing a malicious joke at the expense of his creations. The following quotation, for example, demonstrates Empson's interpretation of the exaltation of the Son (p. 102):

> If the Son had inherently held this position from before the creation of all angels, why has it been officially withheld from him till this day, and still more, why have the angels not previously been told that he was the agent of their creation? ... to give no reason at all for the Exaltation makes it appear a challenge, intended to outrage a growing intellectual dissatisfaction among the angels with the claims of God.

Empson presents serious challenges to the heart of the poem, which have provoked a variety of answers. It is possible, for example, to claim that Milton's purpose was to justify God's ways, and not the existence of God himself, and that, lacking any faith in God, Empson follows the fallen characters in the poem and is not prepared to be obedient unless there is some evident reward. (The poem includes several examples of obedience without immediate reward.)

Dennis Burden's argument is persuasive: that God is presented as loving and just, but without the arbitrariness of affection which pity would involve (*The Logical Epic*, p. 35):

> To ascribe pity to God ... would, since God has created Man's world and Man's nature, indict that providence which *Paradise Lost* is written to assert. Milton is very insistent on this need to regard without pity those episodes representing God's anger and justice. One of Raphael's difficulties in recounting the Fall of the angels to Adam is the necessity for the story to he told and listened to without pity.

It may be significant that, although Empson's revised edition of *Milton's God* (CUP, 1981) includes an appendix on the reaction of other critics to Empson's argument, it makes no reference to Burden's book.

CRITICS ON PREDESTINATION

Burden's description of a just, impartial God is not dissimilar from that of critics who have attempted to defend Milton's God on the grounds that (unlike, for example, the God of the Calvinist tradition) God in *Paradise Lost* does not predestine the fall of man, nor does he deny grace to anyone. Milton's God shows neither arbitrary pity nor favouritism, and the poem does not, therefore, include the notion of an 'elect' whose salvation is predetermined by God. God's speech in Book III emphasises that man is responsible for his own fate (lines 120–5) and that, after the fall, salvation is equally dependent upon individual choice and action (lines 191–3).

Milton's prose and poetry continually asserted the need for faith to be explicit, and his statements on salvation in *De Doctrina Christiana*, his principal theological treatise, reinforce the impression of his commitment to a belief in the need for good works as part of the process of salvation. Christopher Hill, in *Milton and the English Revolution* (Faber, 1977, p. 276) cites this passage from *De Doctrina Christiana* as evidence of Milton's position: 'A true and living faith cannot exist without works ... Those who persevere, not those who are elect, are said to attain salvation.' *Paradise Lost* also treats salvation in this fashion, although the issue is somewhat obscured by Milton's use of the word 'elect'. In *De Doctrina Christiana* he defines the elect as those who believe and continue in the faith, and it is used in this sense in most of the instances in which it occurs in *Paradise Lost*. Thus, for example, the angels who remain loyal to God are described as elect (Book III lines 135–8):

> Thus while God spake, ambrosial fragrance filled
> All heaven, and in the blessed spirits elect
> Sense of new joy ineffable diffused.

Milton is careful to present this group of angels as having achieved election by exercising their own free choice in deciding to remain faithful. This usage of 'elect', therefore, corresponds exactly to that of *De Doctrina Christiana*, implying the act of choosing rather than the passive state of being chosen. The difficulty is that Milton also uses the word in its more usual sense twice in *Paradise Lost*. In the final book Michael describes to Adam the flight of the Israelites from Egypt (Book XII lines 214–16):

> the race elect
> Safe towards Canaan from the shore advance
> Through the wild desert

And in Book III, in the midst of his declaration of the doctrine of salvation, Milton's God creates an exception to his own rule: 'Some I have chosen of peculiar grace / Elect above the rest; so is my will' (lines 183–4). This latter passage seems to refer to those individuals who, like Milton himself, had been singled out by God to enact some special role in the divine scheme. Milton continued to believe in his own personal election, as he had once believed in the special favour which God extended to his chosen English nation; but this did not absolve him, and others similarly elected by God, from the obligation to do good works on earth. Indeed, since God's chosen nation had decided not to carry through the Revolution to its full course, the obligation for Milton to remain personally firm was all the stronger.

Milton continually contrives his poem in a way which suggests that, although God may know of the outcome of Satan's temptation, the details of the process are left obscured. Thus, for example, in Book III God talks of the future fall of man, but he does not discriminate between the separate falls of Eve and Adam, nor indicate the precise means by which Satan will bring about this fall. It seems as if the outcome of events is foreseen by God, but the motives and arguments which lead to these events are not predetermined. In a work which operates to such a large extent through debates, this means that a considerable part of the most interesting intellectual activity within *Paradise Lost* is made to seem to take place outside God's prediction. In *Milton's God* Empson observed that (p. 36):

> Milton regularly presents a fall as due to an intellectually interesting temptation, such that a cool judge may feel actual doubt whether the fall was not the best thing to do in the circumstances.

These 'intellectually interesting' temptations are inventions on Milton's part which are made to seem quite independent of God's predestined plan. They are a product of the self-awareness and freedom which Milton (and, by implication, Milton's God) gives to his characters, and which, if abused, leads not to a liberation from God but to a new kind of self-enslavement. What God says of man in Book III – 'I formed them free, and free they must remain, / Till they enthrall themselves' (lines 124–5) – anticipates in terms of the narrative (although in biblical terms it succeeds it) the speech of Abdiel to Satan, one of the most significant definitions in the poem (Book VI lines 178–81):

> This is servitude,
> To serve the unwise, or him who hath rebelled
> Against his worthier, as thine now serve thee,
> Thy self not free, but to thy self enthralled.

Paradise Lost offers a choice between, on the one hand, the true freedom of obedience to God and faith in God's providence, and, on the other hand, a life without God, which gives the illusion of freedom but is, in fact, the servitude of self-enslavement. One of the consequences of the fall is that a new distinction has to be made between 'liberty' and 'licence', the very distinction which was so significant in the debates during the English Revolution. 'Liberty', for Milton, involves obedience to God and conformity to God's ordered scheme; 'licentious' behaviour is the signal of the attempt to live outside this divine scheme, and leads ultimately to anarchy.

Milton's principal difficulty in working this discrimination between licence and liberty into the fabric of *Paradise Lost* is that his definition of liberty is static and therefore potentially less interesting than conventional

notions of freedom. Adam, at the close of the poem (Book XII
lines 561–4), says that he has learned:

> that to obey is best,
> And love with fear the only God, to walk
> As in his presence, ever to observe
> His providence, and on him sole depend

But it is difficult to place such a definition of liberty at the centre of an
epic poem and still maintain the interest of the reader. A great many
critics have raised their particular version of this problem, which is a
variant of the charge that Satan is too attractive to fail. Molly Mahood,
taking Milton's *Paradise Regained* (1671) into her consideration, argues
that 'there is little to show how "Heav'nly love shal outdoo Hellish hate"
[*Paradise Lost*, Book III line 298], small demonstration of that
"unexampl'd love" which compels the Son to suffer such an ordeal' (in A.
Rudrum, ed., *Milton*, Macmillan, 1970, p. 245). G.A. Wilkes (*English
Renaissance Studies*, Oxford University Press, 1980, pp. 272–4) holds that:

> The loss of paradise is powerfully brought home to us; the process of redemption
> and restoration may seem by contrast a mechanical victory … Certainly the new
> Eden promised is to be superior to the Eden that has been lost … But the
> realization of this is paradise outside the scheme of the poem.

Dennis Burden (*The Logical Epic*, p. 180) is driven to defend the overall
scheme of the poem in this way:

> The climax of Book XII, the Incarnation, is not reached with any notable growth
> or development. The promises about the Messiah are not disposed in any
> significant order, nor do the types of Christ get bigger and better types … Like the
> account of the war in Heaven in Book VI, Book XII offers for the most part less
> logical challenge and opportunity, and the lacklustre response which is all that it
> arouses in most of its readers shows how important are the logic and tautness of
> the poem elsewhere.

However, it could be argued that this sense of disappointment,
experienced by many readers of the poem, is deliberately contrived
by Milton. It is consistent with the reversal of expectation endured
by characters within the poem, and is part of a reworking of epic
convention which is so radical (see Literary Background on The Epic

Tradition) that further development of the genre after Milton became impossible.

CRITICISM OF *PARADISE LOST* IN THE LATE TWENTIETH CENTURY

The practice of literary criticism underwent a significant transformation in the final quarter of the twentieth century. Put simply, there were two distinct movements. The first was a challenge to the idea that the syllabus of English Literature is fixed, and that certain texts should be required reading, and have the status of 'classics'. The second saw a growing argument that all texts, whatever their provenance, inevitably carry some bias, whether from politics, social class, gender or race, and that all readings of texts will carry similar bias on the part of the readers.

Milton criticism has been affected by these movements, and a good synopsis of the movement of critical practice in respect of the study of Milton is provided by Annabel Patterson in her introduction to *John Milton* (Longman, 1992), a collection of essays edited by her.

Terry Eagleton, a leading figure in recent debates over literature, and himself a Marxist critic, makes the following observation on the nature of the English Studies syllabus in his influential and very readable book *Literary Theory: An Introduction* (Blackwell, 1983, p. 214):

> Nobody is likely to be dismissed from an academic job for trying on a little semiotic analysis of Edmund Spenser; they are likely to be shown the door ... if they question whether the 'tradition' from Spenser to Shakespeare and Milton is the best or only way to carve up discourse into a syllabus.

In other words it is one thing to try new techniques (such as semiotics) on an 'established' writer (such as Milton's famous predecessor Spenser), but it is quite another to question whether any writer actually is 'established' or not.

Eagleton goes on to exemplify the way in which bias and ideology operate in literary criticism. For Eagleton, no reading of a text can be politically or ideologically neutral. This is borne out by what we have seen already with respect to criticism of Milton's language. F.R. Leavis was noticing something about Milton's use of language (not necessarily noticing it accurately) but failing to relate that to a wider set of his own assumptions, not least Leavis's own particular prejudices. Similarly, it is not surprising that Empson, an atheist, should find Milton's God unpalatable.

It has always been possible for readers to be prejudiced against Milton's writings because of what they believed about Milton the man: his politics, or his views on marriage, or what they had heard about his relationship with his daughters. The influence of Robert Graves's novel *Wife to Mr Milton* (1942) may account for some of these views. It ought to be the case that evaluation of the quality of a work should operate separately from any evaluation of its writer, but all too often the two become confused. In fact, it would seem that Milton himself did not separate the writer from the writing – see the extract from his *An Apology for Smectymnuus* reproduced on p. 69 of this Note; but much recent criticism has attempted to do just that. In the past fifty years, critics have started to pose questions of the type 'Did Milton write *Paradise Lost*?' Such a question does not imply a belief that somebody else may have written the poem (as some would seek to attribute Shakespeare's plays to Christopher Marlowe or Francis Bacon), but rather that the poem had no real 'author' at all, instead being an inevitable product of the historical moment of England after the Restoration of the monarchy. Two critics in particular have shifted attention away from the notion that there exists a single author for any text, and towards the idea that literary texts are constructed by society as a whole: the philosophers Roland Barthes and Michel Foucault produced influential essays on this matter, respectively, 'The Death of the Author' (1968) and 'What is an Author?' (1969). At this point the boundaries between literary criticism and philosophy become blurred. For further reading in this area, see the entry on 'Author' in Martin Gray's *A Dictionary of Literary Terms* (York Handbooks, Longman, 1992).

Influential among those writers who have examined the relationship between Milton's work and his contemporary situation has been the historian Christopher Hill, whose book *Milton and the English Revolution* (Faber, 1977) charts in detail the references in *Paradise Lost* to the politics of the seventeenth century. More recently, Christopher Kendrick pursues a similar investigation in *Milton: A Study in Ideology and Form* (Methuen, 1986) while Laura L. Knoppers, in *Historicizing Milton: Spectacle, Power and Poetry in Restoration England* (University of Georgia Press, 1994), makes a convincing case that the use and frequency of such words as 'restore' and 'joy' in *Paradise Lost* are specific references to the public celebrations which followed the Restoration of Charles II.

One particularly influential form of literary criticism in the twentieth century was **feminism**. This form of criticism is not confined to discussion of texts by women (nor is it the sole province of women critics), but considers the treatment of gender, and of male and female viewpoints, in all texts. Not surprisingly, a great deal of the feminist criticism of *Paradise Lost* is concerned with Milton's presentation of Eve – see, for example, Diane Kelsey McColley's *Milton's Eve* (University of Illinois Press, 1983). However, readers of Books I and II might well wish to reflect upon the way in which Sin is presented in the second Book: is it fair to describe Sin, an abstraction, as a female, or would it be reasonable to regard her as an abused woman? One might also consider the significance of Milton's description of Solomon, in Book I line 444, as 'that uxorious king'. For further reading in this area, two good books containing feminist readings of Milton are Catherine Belsey's *John Milton: Language, Gender and Power* (Blackwell, 1988) and *Milton and the Idea of Woman*, ed. M. Walker (University of Illinois Press, 1988).

Another movement in twentieth-century criticism reflected in the study of Milton is **post-colonialism**. This movement is not simply confined to the study of works produced in countries formerly colonised by European powers, but also considers the presentation of colonialism and imperialism in earlier texts. For example, Emily C. Bartels, in *Spectacles of Strangeness* (University of Pennsylvania Press, 1993), looks at Christopher Marlowe's plays as post-colonial products. J.M. Evans, in *Milton's Imperial Epic* (Cornell University Press, 1996), considers *Paradise Lost* as a text shaped by notions of colonial expansion.

FURTHER READING

WORKS ON *PARADISE LOST*

There are hundreds of books, chapters and articles on *Paradise Lost*. The vast majority of these are concerned with the poem as a whole, not just its opening two Books. Perhaps the most obvious further reading would therefore be to become acquainted with the whole of *Paradise Lost*. Without such an acquaintance these opening Books do not make full sense.

For example, the description of the activities of the fallen angels after Satan's departure in Book II needs to be set against the activities of the angels in heaven in Book III. Similarly, the relationship between Satan, Sin and Death needs to be read in association with the relationships between God and the Son, and between Adam and Eve; and a full appreciation of Satan volunteering to corrupt mankind needs the context of the Son volunteering to redeem mankind.

If reading all of *Paradise Lost* seems too daunting a task, students will find much of interest in Milton's early short poem 'On the Morning of Christ's Nativity', which includes a catalogue of false gods similar to that in Book I of *Paradise Lost*.

The list of secondary reading below includes those titles referred to in earlier sections of this Note, in addition to other influential criticism. For readers wishing to keep abreast of the most recent Milton scholarship, it is worth browsing through *Milton Quarterly*, reading the *Year's Work in English Studies*, or consulting the *Milton Review* Web site at www.urich.edu/~creamer/reviewed.html.

C. Belsey, *John Milton*, Blackwell, 1988

H. Blamires, *Milton's Creation*, Methuen, 1971

F. Blessington, *Paradise Lost and the Classical Epic*, Routledge, 1979

H. Bloom, *A Map of Misreading*, Oxford University Press, 1975

D. Burden, *The Logical Epic*, Routledge, 1967

D. Danielson, *Milton's Good God*, Cambridge University Press, 1982

S. Davies, *Images of Kingship in Paradise Lost*, Columbia University Press, 1983

T.S. Eliot, *On Poetry and Poets*, Faber, 1957

W. Empson, *Milton's God*, Cambridge University Press, revised 1981

J.M. Evans, *Milton's Imperial Epic*, Cornell University Press, 1996

S. Fish, *Surprised by Sin*, University of California Press, 1967

M. Grossman, *Authors to Themselves*, Cambridge University Press, 1987

G. Hunter, *Paradise Lost*, Allen and Unwin, 1980

C. Kendrick, *Milton: A Study in Ideology and Form*, Methuen, 1986

W. Kerrigan, *The Sacred Complex*, Harvard University Press, 1983

L.L. Knoppers, *Historicizing Milton: Spectacle, Power and Poetry in Restoration England*, University of Georgia Press, 1994

C.S. Lewis, *A Preface to Paradise Lost*, Oxford University Press, 1942

D. McColley, *Milton's Eve*, University of Illinois Press, 1982

B. Rajan, *The Lofty Rhyme*, Routledge, 1970

C. Ricks, *Milton's Grand Style*, Oxford University Press, 1963

R. Schwartz, *Remembering and Repeating: Biblical Creation in Paradise Lost*, Cambridge University Press, 1988

J. Webber, *Milton and His Epic Tradition*, University of Washington Press, 1979

SURVEYS OF THE HISTORICAL AND LITERARY BACKGROUND

H. Erskine-Hill and G. Storey (eds), *Revolutionary Prose*, Cambridge University Press, 1983

B. Ford, *The New Pelican Guide to English Literature*, vol. 3, Penguin, 1980

L. Marcus, *Unediting The Renaissance*, Routledge, 1996

D. Morse, *England's Time of Crisis*, Macmillan, 1989

C.W.R.D. Moseley, *Poetic Birth*, Scolar Press, 1991

C. Patrides and R. Waddington (eds), *The Age of Milton*, Manchester University Press, 1980

R. Richardson and G. Ridden (eds), *Freedom and the English Revolution*, Manchester University Press, 1986

G. Ridden, *Studying Milton*, Longman, 1985

MILTON'S LIFE

A. Barker, *Milton and the Puritan Dilemma*, University of Toronto Press, 1942

H. Darbishire (ed.), *The Early Lives of Milton*, Constable, 1932

J. Diekhoff, *Milton on Himself*, Cohen and West, 1939

C. Hill, *Milton and the English Revolution*, Faber, 1977

W.R. Parker, *Milton: A Biography*, Oxford University Press, 1968

W.R. Parker, *Milton's Contemporary Reputation*, Haskell, 1940

A.N. Wilson, *The Life of John Milton*, Oxford University Press, 1983

D. Wolfe, *Milton in the Puritan Revolution*, Nelson, 1941

COLLECTIONS OF CRITICAL ESSAYS

C. Bloom (ed.), *Jacobean Poetry and Prose*, Macmillan, 1988

D. Danielson (ed.), *The Cambridge Guide to Milton*, Cambridge University Press, 1989

F. Kermode (ed.), *The Living Milton*, Routledge, 1960

A. Patterson (ed.), *John Milton*, Longman, 1992

M. Nyquist and M. Ferguson (eds), *Re-Membering Milton*, Methuen, 1987

A. Rudrum (ed.), *Milton*, Macmillan, 1970

M. Walker (ed.), *Milton and the Idea of Woman*, University of Illinois Press, 1988

REFERENCE

W.B. Hunter (ed.), *A Milton Encyclopaedia*, Associated University Press, 1978–80

INTERNET RESOURCES

In addition to books and articles published in print, students of Milton in the twenty-first century are fortunate in having access to a number of scholarly Web sites devoted to the poet.

At www.dartmouth.edu/~milton you will find the Milton Reading Room, which includes editions of Milton's poems and some of his prose works: these are supplied with useful footnotes. The site at www.literature.org and the Project Gutenberg site at www.promo.net/pg include a range of literary texts, including some by Milton. *Milton Review* and the Milton List can be found at www.richmond.edu/~creamer/milton.

Among the benefits of having access to texts by Milton on the Web is that students can search for particular words or phrases, something which is impossible when using a printed text, unless one has a concordance to hand.

Historical events	Milton's life	Literature
		1590 Edmund Spenser, *The Faerie Queene* (Books I-III)
		1596 Spenser, *The Faerie Queene* (Books IV-VI)
		1599 Death of Spenser
	1608 Born on 9 December in Bread Street, London	
		1609 William Shakespeare, *Sonnets*
		1610 Ben Jonson, *The Alchemist*
		1616 Death of Shakespeare
	1620 Attends St Paul's School around this time	
		1621 Birth of Andrew Marvell
1625 Charles I crowned King of England and Ireland	**1625** Begins study at Cambridge University	
1629 Charles dissolves Parliament	**1629** Awarded BA; writes 'Nativity Ode'	**1629** William Davenant, *The Just Italian*
		1631 Death of John Donne
	1632 Writes *L'Allegro* and *Il Penseroso*; 'On Shakespeare' published in the Second Folio edition of Shakespeare's plays	
1633 William Laud appointed Archbishop of Canterbury		**1633** Donne's *Poems* published posthumously

Historical events	Milton's life	Literature
	1634 *Comus* performed (published 1637)	
		1637 Death of Jonson
	1638 Publication of *Lycidas;* Milton travels abroad, meeting Galileo while in Italy	
1639–40 The two Bishops' Wars between Charles I and the Scottish Covenanters end in bankruptcy for Charles I and the establishment of the Long Parliament		
1640 The Long Parliament impeaches Laud; Charles I's principal adviser Strafford is executed		
	1641 Writes a number of anti-prelatical tracts	
1642 Civil War breaks out	**1642** Writes more anti-prelatical pamphlets; marries Mary Powell, who leaves him later in the year	
	1643 Publishes the first of four tracts on divorce which are met with public outcry	**1643** William Prynne, *The Sovereign Power of Parliaments*
1644 Oliver Cromwell leads Parliamentarians to victory at the battle of Marston Moor	**1644** Publishes *Areopagitica* (on freedom of speech), *Of Education* and a second tract on divorce	

Historical events	Milton's life	Literature
1645 Laud is executed; Parliament establishes the New Model Army, which defeats Charles's forces at the battle of Naseby	**1645** Publishes two more pamphlets on divorce and *Poems 1645,* his first collection of poetry; Mary returns	
	1646 Birth of daughter Anne	
1647 Charles is arrested but escapes		**1647** Henry More, *Philosophical Poems*
1648 Charles is re-arrested	**1648** Birth of daughter Mary	
1649 Charles is executed at Whitehall	**1649** Appointed Secretary of Foreign Tongues to the Council of State; writes two tracts on Charles's execution	
	1650 By now almost totally blind	**1650** Marvell, 'An Horatian Ode upon Cromwell's Return from Ireland'; Thomas Hobbes, *De Corpore Politico*
	1651 Writes his official defence of the Commonwealth; birth of son John	**1651** Davenant, *Gondibert*
	1652 Birth of daughter Deborah; death of wife Mary and son John	
1653 Cromwell establishes Protectorate		
	1654 Publishes second defence of the Commonwealth	

Historical events	Milton's life	Literature
	1655 *Defence of Himself*	**1655** Marvell, *First Anniversary of the Government under the Lord Protector*
	1656 Marries Katherine Woodcock	
1657 Cromwell refuses the offer of the crown	**1657** Daughter Katherine born; Andrew Marvell is appointed an assistant to Milton	
1658 Death of Oliver Cromwell; his son Richard succeeds as Lord Protector	**1658** Death of wife Katherine and daughter Katherine	
1659 Richard Cromwell abdicates	**1659** Publishes two tracts on religious freedom	**1659** John Dryden, *Poem upon the Death of His Late Highness Oliver Lord Protector*
1660 Restoration of the monarchy following the collapse of the Protectorate; Charles II becomes King	**1660** Writes a tract in favour of the Commonwealth; following the Restoration, Milton is imprisoned briefly and his books are publicly burned	
		1661 Dryden, *To His Sacred Majesty*
	1663 Marries Elizabeth Minshull	
1666 Great Fire of London		
	1667 Publication of *Paradise Lost* in 10 Books	**1667** Dryden, *Annus Mirabilis*
	1671 Publication of *Paradise Regained* and *Samson Agonistes*	
	1674 Second edition of *Paradise Lost*, in 12 Books; dies on 8 November	

alliteration a sequence of repeated consonantal sounds, usually at the beginning of words or of stressed syllables

allusion a passing reference in a work of literature to something external to the work (such as another work of literature, a legend, a cultural belief or a historical fact)

blank verse unrhymed lines of verse each containing five iambs (iambic pentameters). An iamb is the commonest metrical foot in English verse, consisting of an unstressed syllable followed by a stressed syllable

epic a long narrative poem in an elevated style. Typical epic themes include myth, legend, and the birth and destruction of nations – see Literary Background on The Epic Tradition

epic simile a long simile, sometimes extended over more than twenty lines, which typically interrupts the narrative of a poem, allowing the poet to make detailed comparisons

epigram originally, an inscription on a monument. The term 'epigrammatic' is now used to describe any short poem which has a sharp turn of thought or point, be it witty, amusing or satirical

feminism a tenet of feminist thought is that male ways of perceiving and ordering are 'inscribed' into the prevailing ideology of society. In terms of literary criticism, this can be disclosed by studying language itself, and texts, in order to discover the characteristic assumptions which are inherent in them

flyting versified abuse: a quarrel in poetry between warriors about to do battle

hero in its simplest sense, the chief character in a work of literature. In relation to *Paradise Lost*, Milton uses the term to refer to a person of superhuman ability who leads, and is revered by, his people. Many earlier epics had been the stories of just such men, who were regarded as having saved their nations. Milton is concerned to argue that military prowess is only one form of courage, and that the heroism of the Son in *Paradise Lost* is manifest not in his military valour but in his patient and silent suffering on behalf of all humanity. See also Critical Approaches on Satan & Drama

imagery in its narrowest sense an image is a picture in words – a description of some visible scene or object. More commonly, however, 'imagery' refers to the figurative language in a work of literature, such as metaphors and similes; or all the words which refer to objects and qualities which appeal to the senses and feelings

in medias res (Latin: 'into the middle of things') a phrase describing a common technique of storytelling in which the narrator begins not at the beginning of a story or action, but in the middle, going back to recount earlier events at a later stage, or letting them emerge during the course of the story. This is a convention of the epic, but also occurs in the novel (for example, Emily Brontë's *Wuthering Heights*)

motaphor a departure from literal writing which goes further than a comparison (or simile) between two different things or ideas by fusing them together: one thing is described as being another thing

narrator the person who tells the story. In many works of literature the narrator can be distinguished from the author of a work, and is the fictional person who we choose to accept as having constructed the narrative. In the case of *Paradise Lost*, however, John Milton can be regarded as both author and narrator

oxymoron a figure of speech in which contradictory terms are brought together in what seems at first to be an impossible combination, for example: 'Chained on the burning lake' (Book I line 210). An oxymoron is thus a special form of paradox

panegyric a public speech or poem which wholeheartedly praises someone or something

paradox a bringing together of terms which seem to contradict into a combination which has an underlying meaning, truth or humour

parody an imitation of a specific work of literature or style, devised so as to ridicule its characteristic features. In an extreme form, parody can become so grotesque and ludicrous as to be a travesty

personification a figurative use of language in which things or ideas are treated as if they were human beings, with human attributes and feelings. Examples in *Paradise Lost* include Sin, Death and Chaos: Death is described as if he could feel anger

post-colonialism the varied literatures of the many countries whose political existence has been shaped by the experience of colonialism are seen by post-colonialist critics to share basic characteristics, especially in relation to their use (or non-use) of the language of the colonial power, and the cultural and literary associations attached to that language

rhetoric originally, the art of speaking (and writing) effectively so as to persuade an audience; the term is now often used to cover the whole range of literary and linguistic devices

simile a species of figurative writing involving a direct comparison of one thing to another. Similes typically make use of the words 'like' or 'as'

soliloquy a dramatic convention in which a character speaks directly to the audience, as if thinking aloud about motives, feelings and decisions

symbolism the use of symbols in a work of literature. A symbol is something which represents something else (often an idea or quality) by analogy or association – a writer may use conventional symbols, which form part of a literary or cultural tradition, as well as creating new ones

synecdoche a figure of speech in which a part is used to describe the whole, for example when describing a herd of cattle as 'one hundred head'

tenor and **vehicle** the two components of a metaphor (or simile): the tenor is the subject, and the vehicle the thing itself. For example, if Satan is described as being like a whale, Satan is the vehicle and the whale is the tenor

AUTHOR OF THIS NOTE

Geoff Ridden has worked in higher education for almost thirty years, publishing a substantial number of articles, including regular contributions to the *Milton Quarterly*. His books include *Studying Milton* and *Freedom and the English Revolution*. For most of his working life, he has taught at King Alfred's University College, Winchester, where he is currently Principal Lecturer in the School of Cultural Studies; he has also lectured in Ghana, Norway, Poland and the USA. In his spare time, for the past twenty years, he has been one half of a stand-up comedy duo .

York Notes Advanced (£3.99 each)

Margaret Atwood
Cat's Eye

Margaret Atwood
The Handmaid's Tale

Jane Austen
Mansfield Park

Jane Austen
Persuasion

Jane Austen
Pride and Prejudice

Alan Bennett
Talking Heads

William Blake
*Songs of Innocence and of
Experience*

Charlotte Brontë
Jane Eyre

Emily Brontë
Wuthering Heights

Angela Carter
Nights at the Circus

Geoffrey Chaucer
*The Franklin's Prologue and
Tale*

Geoffrey Chaucer
The Miller's Prologue and Tale

Geoffrey Chaucer
*Prologue To the Canterbury
Tales*

Geoffrey Chaucer
*The Wife of Bath's Prologue
and Tale*

Samuel Taylor Coleridge
Selected Poems

Joseph Conrad
Heart of Darkness

Daniel Defoe
Moll Flanders

Charles Dickens
Great Expectations

Charles Dickens
Hard Times

Emily Dickinson
Selected Poems

John Donne
Selected Poems

Carol Ann Duffy
Selected Poems

George Eliot
Middlemarch

George Eliot
The Mill on the Floss

T.S. Eliot
Selected Poems

F. Scott Fitzgerald
The Great Gatsby

E.M. Forster
A Passage to India

Brian Friel
Translations

Thomas Hardy
The Mayor of Casterbridge

Thomas Hardy
The Return of the Native

Thomas Hardy
Selected Poems

Thomas Hardy
Tess of the d'Urbervilles

Seamus Heaney
*Selected Poems from Opened
Ground*

Nathaniel Hawthorne
The Scarlet Letter

Kazuo Ishiguro
The Remains of the Day

Ben Jonson
The Alchemist

James Joyce
Dubliners

John Keats
Selected Poems

Christopher Marlowe
Doctor Faustus

Arthur Miller
Death of a Salesman

John Milton
Paradise Lost Books I & II

Toni Morrison
Beloved

Sylvia Plath
Selected Poems

Alexander Pope
*Rape of the Lock and other
poems*

William Shakespeare
Antony and Cleopatra

William Shakespeare
As You Like It

William Shakespeare
Hamlet

William Shakespeare
King Lear

William Shakespeare
Measure for Measure

William Shakespeare
The Merchant of Venice

William Shakespeare
A Midsummer Night's Dream

William Shakespeare
Much Ado About Nothing

William Shakespeare
Othello

William Shakespeare
Richard II

William Shakespeare
Romeo and Juliet

William Shakespeare
The Taming of the Shrew

William Shakespeare
The Tempest

William Shakespeare
Twelfth Night

William Shakespeare
The Winter's Tale

George Bernard Shaw
Saint Joan

Mary Shelley
Frankenstein

Jonathan Swift
*Gulliver's Travels and A Modest
Proposal*

Alfred, Lord Tennyson
Selected Poems

Alice Walker
The Color Purple

Oscar Wilde
*The Importance of Being
Earnest*

Tennessee Williams
A Streetcar Named Desire

John Webster
The Duchess of Malfi

Virginia Woolf
To the Lighthouse

W.B. Yeats
Selected Poems

FUTURE TITLES IN THE YORK NOTES SERIES

Jane Austen
Emma

Jane Austen
Sense and Sensibility

Samuel Beckett
Waiting for Godot and
Endgame

Louis de Bernières
Captain Corelli's Mandolin

Charlotte Brontë
Villette

Caryl Churchill
Top Girls and *Cloud Nine*

Charles Dickens
Bleak House

T.S. Eliot
The Waste Land

Thomas Hardy
Jude the Obscure

Homer
The Iliad

Homer
The Odyssey

Aldous Huxley
Brave New World

D.H. Lawrence
Selected Poems

Christopher Marlowe
Edward II

George Orwell
Nineteen Eighty-four

Jean Rhys
Wide Sargasso Sea

William Shakespeare
Henry IV Pt I

William Shakespeare
Henry IV Part II

William Shakespeare
Macbeth

William Shakespeare
Richard III

Tom Stoppard
Arcadia and *Rosencrantz and
Guildenstern are Dead*

Virgil
The Aeneid

Jeanette Winterson
*Oranges are Not the Only
Fruit*

Tennessee Williams
Cat on a Hot Tin Roof

Metaphysical Poets

OTHER TITLES

GCSE and equivalent levels (£3.50 each)

Maya Angelou
I Know Why the Caged Bird Sings

Jane Austen
Pride and Prejudice

Alan Ayckbourn
Absent Friends

Elizabeth Barrett Browning
Selected Poems

Robert Bolt
A Man for All Seasons

Harold Brighouse
Hobson's Choice

Charlotte Brontë
Jane Eyre

Emily Brontë
Wuthering Heights

Shelagh Delaney
A Taste of Honey

Charles Dickens
David Copperfield

Charles Dickens
Great Expectations

Charles Dickens
Hard Times

Charles Dickens
Oliver Twist

Roddy Doyle
Paddy Clarke Ha Ha Ha

George Eliot
Silas Marner

George Eliot
The Mill on the Floss

Anne Frank
The Diary of Anne Frank

William Golding
Lord of the Flies

Oliver Goldsmith
She Stoops To Conquer

Willis Hall
The Long and the Short and the Tall

Thomas Hardy
Far from the Madding Crowd

Thomas Hardy
The Mayor of Casterbridge

Thomas Hardy
Tess of the d'Urbervilles

Thomas Hardy
The Withered Arm and other Wessex Tales

L.P. Hartley
The Go-Between

Seamus Heaney
Selected Poems

Susan Hill
I'm the King of the Castle

Barry Hines
A Kestrel for a Knave

Louise Lawrence
Children of the Dust

Harper Lee
To Kill a Mockingbird

Laurie Lee
Cider with Rosie

Arthur Miller
The Crucible

Arthur Miller
A View from the Bridge

Robert O'Brien
Z for Zachariah

Frank O'Connor
My Oedipus Complex and Other Stories

George Orwell
Animal Farm

J.B. Priestley
An Inspector Calls

J.B. Priestley
When We Are Married

Willy Russell
Educating Rita

Willy Russell
Our Day Out

J.D. Salinger
The Catcher in the Rye

William Shakespeare
Henry IV Part 1

William Shakespeare
Henry V

William Shakespeare
Julius Caesar

William Shakespeare
Macbeth

William Shakespeare
The Merchant of Venice

William Shakespeare
A Midsummer Night's Dream

William Shakespeare
Much Ado About Nothing

William Shakespeare
Romeo and Juliet

William Shakespeare
The Tempest

William Shakespeare
Twelfth Night

George Bernard Shaw
Pygmalion

Mary Shelley
Frankenstein

R.C. Sherriff
Journey's End

Rukshana Smith
Salt on the Snow

John Steinbeck
Of Mice and Men

Robert Louis Stevenson
Dr Jekyll and Mr Hyde

Jonathan Swift
Gulliver's Travels

Robert Swindells
Daz 4 Zoe

Mildred D. Taylor
Roll of Thunder, Hear My Cry

Mark Twain
Huckleberry Finn

James Watson
Talking in Whispers

Edith Wharton
Ethan Frome

William Wordsworth
Selected Poems

A Choice of Poets

Mystery Stories of the Nineteenth Century including The Signalman

Nineteenth Century Short Stories

Poetry of the First World War

Six Women Poets

NOTES

Notes

NOTES